F. Scott Fitzgerald's
Taste of France

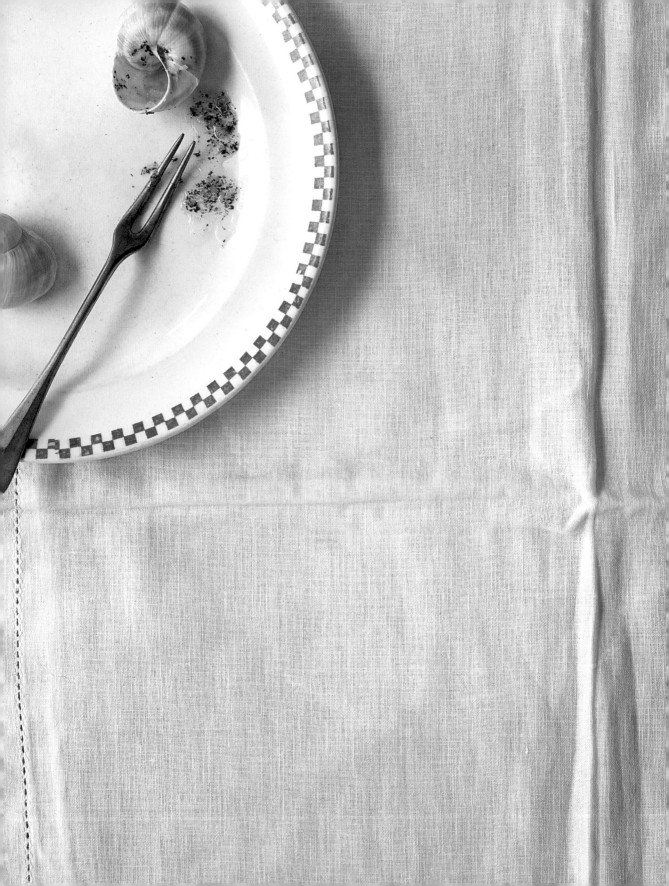

F. Scott Fitzgerald's
Taste of France

Recipes inspired by the cafés and bars
of Fitzgerald's Paris and the Riviera
in the 1920s

Carol Hilker

CICO BOOKS
LONDON NEW YORK
www.rylandpeters.com

Published in 2016 by CICO Books
An imprint of Ryland Peters & Small Ltd
20–21 Jockey's Fields   341 E 116th St
London WC1R 4BW   New York, NY 10029

www.rylandpeters.com

10 9 8 7 6 5 4 3 2 1

A CIP catalog record for this book is available from the Library
of Congress and the British Library.

ISBN: 978 1 78249 378 5

Printed in China

Editors: Gillian Haslam and Nathan Joyce
Designer: Louise Leffler
Photographer: Alex Luck
Stylist: Luis Peral
Food stylist: Sue Henderson
Food styling assistants: Loic Parisot and Sian Henle

Editor: Miriam Catley
Art director: Sally Powell
Head of production: Patricia Harrington
Publishing manager: Penny Craig
Publisher: Cindy Richards

Contents

Introduction

There aren't many people who get through adolescence without being required to read F. Scott Fitzgerald's *The Great Gatsby* in high school. But most people who read it discover not only a good story, but vivid, vibrant characters. That's because Scott Fitzgerald was equally proficient at creating characters as he was at chronicling the world he knew—the excesses of the 1920s and the perils of basking in the glow of early success.

Above: Fitzgerald and his wife Zelda on the French Riviera in 1926. Opposite: Fitzgerald photographed in around 1925, every inch the successful young author.

Fitzgerald married Zelda Sayre and they had one child, Frances Scott, known as "Scottie". In 1924 the family moved to Paris, becoming part of the growing American expatriate community of writers and artists. Although both the Fitzgeralds found themselves back in America sporadically, they would remain for the most part in France until 1931, and undoubtedly spent their most treasured years there. They moved between Paris and the Riviera—Cannes, Antibes, and various stops along the way.

This collection of recipes is an homage to F. Scott and Zelda Fitzgerald and their travels. You'll find a little of Fitzgerald, and some of his fellow Americans in Paris and the Riviera—Gertrude Stein, James Joyce, and Ernest Hemingway amongst them—and a lot of the food and drink that nourished them. There are classic French dishes that you can still order today in the cafés and brasseries of the city, and American dishes that were adopted and adapted by the French. And of course no book of this kind would be complete without recipes for some of the favorite cocktails of Fitzgerald and his friends—excessive drinking made the Fitzgeralds both the most unpredictable but also the liveliest of dinner guests.

In addition, there are special features on some of the history behind the food, from traditional café culture to Parisian cocktail bars staffed by American mixologists escaping Prohibition, the great French chefs who gave birth to France's classic cookery, and the musicians and performers who brought jazz to Europe and in doing so broke down barriers between the old world and the new.

The Jazz Age of the 1920s is undeniably one of the most romanticized periods in literature. In his novels and short stories—particularly in *The Great Gatsby*—Scott Fitzgerald successfully and quite accidentally became the voice of a generation, chronicling a now-iconic period of lush fantasy, excess, and debauchery. Travel back in time to a France where bob haircuts and grandma's cocktail jewelry were as cool as the fruit cocktail. Welcome to the Fitzgerald ex-pat food tour.

A Note on Measurements

Both British (metric) and American (imperial and US cups) measurements and ingredients are included in these recipes for your convenience. However, it is important to work with only one set of measurements and not alternate between the two within a recipe.

Spoon measurements:
1 tablespoon = 15ml
1 dessertspoon = 10ml
1 teaspoon = 5ml
All spoon measurements should be level unless specified otherwise.

All eggs are medium (UK) or large (US) unless specified as large, in which case US extra-large should be used. Uncooked or partially cooked eggs should not be served to the very old, frail, young children, pregnant women, or those with compromized immune systems.

Chapter One
Breakfast

Fitzgerald's Ham and Egg Breakfast

Fitzgerald and Hemingway enjoyed a big American-style breakfast together at a hotel in Lyon, France, as documented by Hemingway in his memoir *A Moveable Feast*. The pair were about to embark on a road trip together in Fitzgerald's small Renault from Lyon to Paris in the early 1920s. The trip would be a challenge because, it turned out, the vehicle was without a roof.

1½ tablespoons unsalted butter

2-lb/900-g uncooked piece of ham, chopped into bite-sized pieces

10 eggs

2 tablespoons milk or cream

1 teaspoon *fleur de sel* or coarse sea salt

¼ teaspoon freshly ground black pepper

1½ cups/135 g grated sharp/mature Cheddar cheese

⅓ cup/15 g freshly chopped chives

SERVES 4–6

Heat the butter in a large non-stick skillet/frying pan over medium heat. Add the ham and sauté until browned. Remove when cooked and set aside.

Meanwhile, in a large bowl, whisk together the eggs, milk or cream, salt, and pepper. Pour into the pan and cook for about 4–5 minutes, stirring occasionally, to desired doneness, adding the cheese and chives just before the eggs are set.

Serve with lots of black coffee and a baguette with jam.

Croque Monsieur and Croque Madame

This French classic first made its appearance in French cafés in the 1910s and gained popularity as a quick snack. It was a favorite of Proust who mentioned it in his work, *In Search of Lost Time*. This decadent grilled ham and cheese uses brioche and grated Gruyère cheese, and is then topped with a béchamel sauce before broiling/grilling. You can modernize this classic by making it with a large pretzel or pretzel buns in place of the brioche.

6 tablespoons/85 g butter

4 tablespoons all-purpose/plain flour

2 cups/475 ml whole milk

¼ teaspoon ground nutmeg

1 bay leaf

8 slices of brioche or pretzel bread

8 oz/225 g thinly sliced ham

8 oz/225 g grated Gruyère cheese, plus extra ½ cup/60 g grated for the topping

salt and freshly ground black pepper

4 fried eggs, for a Croque Madame (optional)

SERVES 4

Melt 4 tablespoons of the butter in a small saucepan over low-medium heat. Add the flour and stir for about 1½ minutes, then gradually whisk in the milk. Add the nutmeg and bay leaf. Increase the heat to medium-high and boil until the sauce thickens, whisking constantly for about 2–3 minutes. Add salt and pepper and set aside.

Preheat the broiler/grill.

Place 4 slices of brioche or pretzel bread on the work surface. Top each with ham and grated Gruyère. Top with the remaining bread slices.

Melt the remaining 2 tablespoons of butter in a small pan. Heat a large heavy skillet/frying pan over low heat. Brush the sandwiches with melted butter. Place in the skillet/frying pan and cook until deep golden brown, about 2 minutes each side. Transfer to a small baking sheet.

Spoon the sauce over the top of each sandwich, then sprinkle over the grated cheese, and place under the broiler/grill. Cook until the cheese begins to brown, about 2 minutes, then serve immediately.

For a Croque Madame, fry the eggs while the sandwiches are under the broiler/grill. Serve each sandwich with an egg on top, sunny side up.

Pastry Pigs
(Saucisses Feuilletées)

Jay Gatsby was a particular fan of these dainty little sausages delightfully wrapped in puff pastry and served them at a big bash he threw in *The Great Gatsby*. Had the Fitzgeralds been enjoying them while on one of their many holidays in France, they would have ordered them as *saucisses feuilletées* at any given restaurant in Paris. These little snacks are easy to make and delicious. They make the perfect start to an early afternoon brunch.

1 sheet of puff pastry (store-bought or homemade)

9 thin sausages or kosher hot dogs

1 egg yolk, beaten

Dijon or wholegrain mustard, to serve

MAKES 9 OR 18 HALVES

Roll the puff pastry into a 12-in/30-cm square, then cut into nine 4-in/10-cm squares.

Roll each sausage in a pastry square. Press the pastry around the sausages, keeping a 1-in/2.5-cm border along the side. Brush some of the egg yolk on the top and sides of the roll and seal the pastry around the sausage. Cut off the excess pastry along the border. If you plan to serve these as hors d'oeuvres, cut each roll in half, so one end is open. Arrange the sausage rolls on a baking sheet lined with baking parchment and place in the freezer for 30 minutes.

Preheat the oven to 400°F (200°C) Gas 6.

Remove the sausage rolls from the freezer and bake in the preheated oven for 20–25 minutes or until puffed and golden. Serve with Dijon or wholegrain mustard.

Peaches and Biscuits

In the summer of 1920, three months after their wedding, the Fitzgeralds decided to flee the quaint Connecticut honeymoon cottage they had been renting. Zelda had become homesick for Montgomery, Alabama, and longed for "peaches and biscuits for breakfast", so the pair embarked on a roadtrip aboard the clapped-out car they had christened "The Rolling Junk" to Zelda's family home. Try this delicious buttermilk biscuit recipe with peach bourbon jam.

Buttermilk Biscuits

2 cups/260 g all-purpose/plain flour, plus extra for dusting

2 teaspoons baking powder

1½ teaspoons fleur de sel or coarse sea salt

1 teaspoon sugar

½ teaspoon baking soda/bicarbonate of soda

8 tablespoons/115 g cold unsalted butter, cut into ½-in/1-cm cubes

1 cup/235 ml cold buttermilk

MAKES 8

Preheat the oven to 425°F (220°C) Gas 7. Set the rack in the center of the oven. Grease a baking sheet or line with a silicone baking mat.

Whisk the dry ingredients together in a bowl. Add the butter pieces and toss to just coat them in the flour mixture. Place the bowl in the freezer for 10 minutes.

Using a pastry blender or two knives and working quickly to avoid softening the butter, cut the butter into the dry ingredients until its consistency is a little larger than pea-sized pieces. Drizzle in the buttermilk and stir just until it comes together as a moist, ragged dough. Work the dough as little as possible.

Generously dust a work surface with flour. Scrape the dough out on to the surface and dust the top with more flour. Using floured hands, gently pat the dough into a circle 1 in/2.5 cm thick.

Using a 2½-in/6-cm round cutter dipped in flour, cut out as many biscuits as possible (press straight down through the dough—do not twist the cutter, or the biscuits will not rise properly). Transfer the biscuits to the prepared baking sheet, spacing them at least 1 in/2.5 cm apart. Gather the scraps into a ball, pat it into a circle, and cut out more biscuits. Repeat as needed until you have 8 in total. Discard any remaining dough (after rolling it twice, it will have lost its potential to rise).

Place the baking sheet in the preheated oven and bake for 15–16 minutes, until the biscuits have risen and are golden brown on top. Transfer to a wire rack to cool slightly before serving.

Peach Bourbon Jam

8–10 peaches (you need 3½ lb/
1.5 kg total weight)

3 cups/700 g sugar

pinch of salt

4 tablespoons freshly squeezed
lemon juice

1 vanilla bean, cut in half lengthwise,
then cut into 1-in/2.5-cm pieces

1¾ oz/55 g low-sugar pectin

4 tablespoons bourbon

1 teaspoon almond extract

MAKES 4–6 JARS, DEPENDING ON SIZE

Blanch the peaches in boiling water for 30 seconds, then submerge them in an ice bath. This will help the skins to slip off easily. Cut the skinned peaches into ¼-in/5-mm pieces and discard the pits.

Put the peaches, sugar, salt, lemon juice, and chopped vanilla bean into a large non-reactive pot (stainless steel is good). Let sit for 30 minutes.

Mash the peaches with a potato masher, until they are well mashed and the ingredients are completely incorporated. If necessary, stir until the sugar has dissolved.

Set the pan over medium-high heat and bring the peach mixture to a rolling boil, stirring frequently to prevent scorching. Boil for 1 minute, then add the pectin. Bring the jam to a rolling boil once more, stirring constantly, and boil for exactly 1 minute.

Remove the jam from heat. Stir in the bourbon and almond extract, then remove the vanilla bean pieces. Ladle the hot jam into sterilized jars and screw on the lids.

The jam will keep in the fridge for up to 2 weeks.

Americans in Paris

"It's not so much what France gave me—so much—it was what she never took away." Gertrude Stein

The beginning of the American expat movement largely came about because of Prohibition, the constitutional ban on the manufacture, sale, or possession of alcoholic drinks that Americans endured between 1920 and 1933. Like a ripple effect, the American artists that migrated to Paris encouraged other artists from all over the world to relocate there as well. In fact, so many Americans were making their way to Paris that various American newspapers such as the *Chicago Tribune* and *The New York Times* ran American versions of French local news in their French-American newspapers. Paris became a place where thousands flocked and countless works of arts were created, many novels were inspired, and some of the best songs were written. It was a momentous time in modern art.

Americans and artists of other nationalities, including Sherwood Anderson, Ezra Pound, Ernest Hemingway, Gertrude Stein, James Joyce, Pablo Picasso, Aaron Copland, Henry Miller, Sylvia Beach, George Gershwin, Cole Porter, Charlie Chaplin, and of course the Fitzgeralds, among countless others, were flocking to France to experience the richness of a country that nurtured the arts. A place where one could eat and drink cheaply, whether in a bustling city, a quaint seaside town, or in the picturesque, lazy countryside.

When Zelda Fitzgerald found out she was pregnant in May 1921, the couple traveled to Europe in the first of many sporadic stays. During their stay at the Hôtel Saint-James et d'Albany in Paris, the couple made their presence known and began their reign as boisterous troublemakers. After antics that involved tying the elevator to the gate on their floor and too many nights of raucous partying—they were kicked out of the hotel, and "found the City of Light a bore and a disappointment because they knew no one there". After being asked to leave, they later set up shop in a Parisian apartment on Rue de Tilsitt where Zelda eventually gave birth to their daughter Scottie. After Scottie's birth, they headed home to America, but not for long.

A few years had gone by and the Fitzgeralds watched as many of their peers took off for France via ocean liners or jets. Bored with Alabama and tired of New York, the couple longed for adventure. Fitzgerald had experienced great success with his first novel, *This Side of Paradise*, and was ready to work on his second. Seeking tranquility for his work, the Fitzgeralds returned to France in the spring of 1924.

Not just Americans: Irish author James Joyce came to Paris in 1920 and stayed for 20 years.

After a quick stay in Paris, they traveled to the French Riviera and lived in the Villa Marie in Valescure.

In Paris in May 1925, Fitzgerald met Ernest Hemingway, then unknown outside the expat literary circle. They formed a friendship based largely on Fitzgerald's admiration for Hemingway's personality and genius. The friendship was a long-lasting one, although it had its ups and downs. Zelda and Ernest never clicked, but Scott never relented in his respect for Hemingway.

In Paris, Fitzgerald spent his days writing and his nights drinking. Sometimes he spent his days drinking as well. Fitzgerald spent time at Gertrude Stein's salon, meeting and collaborating with other artists and writers—many of whom served as inspiration for characters in his books.

James Joyce's Hot Chocolate and Café au Lait

James Joyce emigrated to Paris in 1920 and resolved to finish *Ulysses*, aided by a substantial grant from his benefactor. As well as living the high life, Joyce spent a lot of time at home writing. For the early mornings and late nights that entailed, Joyce would treat himself to a homemade hot chocolate or a café au lait.

Hot Chocolate

3 cups/710 ml whole milk

1 cup/235 ml boiling water

¼ cup/25 g unsweetened cocoa powder (Joyce's brand of choice was Droste)

pinch of salt

3 tablespoons sugar

1 teaspoon vanilla extract

SERVES 4

Scald the milk in a pan over low-medium heat until it is bubbling and just starting to rise, then remove from the heat. Boil the water in a kettle.

In a medium pan, combine the boiled water, cocoa, salt, and sugar. Whisk together thoroughly, to ensure there are no lumps. Add the hot milk to the pan and place over low heat. Stir gently for 2–3 minutes to heat thoroughly.

Remove the pan from the heat and stir in the vanilla extract. Pour into cups to serve.

Café au Lait

1 cup/80 g freshly ground coffee (French Roast, or anything bold and flavorful)

4¼ cups/1 liter hot/boiled water

3 cups/710 ml whole milk

2 teaspoons sugar (optional)

SERVES 4

Place the coffee in a heatproof coffee pot and pour the water over it. Allow to brew for 4–5 minutes. While the coffee brews, scald the milk in a small pan over low heat. Heat the milk carefully—you want to make sure there is no foam.

Mix equal parts of scalded milk and strained coffee in large cups or bowls. If you wish, add sugar to serve.

The Bloody Mary

The Bloody Mary cocktail was invented in the 1920s by an American bartender named Fernand Petiot who worked at Harry's New York Bar in Paris, a common haunt of Fitzgerald and Hemingway. This drink became an essential ritual for those requiring a hair of the dog the morning after!

ice

8 fl oz/225 ml vodka

12 fl oz/340 ml tomato juice

2 fl oz/60 ml freshly squeezed
lemon juice

12 dashes of Worcestershire sauce

2 drops of Tabasco sauce

sea salt and freshly ground
black pepper

4 lemon wedges

4 celery stalks

SERVES 4

Fill 4 highball glasses two-thirds full with ice. Place all the liquids and salt and pepper in a cocktail shaker half-filled with ice and give it 5 or 6 good shakes. Strain into the highball glasses. Garnish with lemon wedges and celery to serve.

Chapter Two
Luncheon

Gloria's Tomato Sandwich and Lemonade

French Deviled Egg Salad Sandwiches

Caviar Sandwiches and Champagne

Oscar Wilde's Cucumber Finger Sandwiches

Gertrude Stein's Roast Beef Picnic Sandwich

Sara Murphy's Creamed Corn Risotto
with Poached Eggs

Cervelats and Mustard Sauce

Pot au Feu

Steak Tartare, or Steak à l'Americaine

Gloria's Tomato Sandwich and Lemonade

Fitzgerald's second novel, *The Beautiful and Damned*, is centered around Anthony Patch, and his wife Gloria. It is said that the novel is a depiction of the tumultuous relationship between the Fitzgeralds. In a lighter moment in the novel, we find Gloria eating a lunch that Zelda Fitzgerald was also fond of: a tomato sandwich.

Gloria's Tomato Sandwich

8 slices of French country-style bread

2 large garlic cloves, halved widthwise

4 tomatoes, 2 halved and 2 thinly sliced

olive oil

fleur de sel or coarse sea salt

mayonnaise (optional)

½ cup/100 g goat cheese

handful of arugula/rocket (optional)

1 Vidalia (or sweet) onion, sliced into thin rings

freshly ground black pepper

MAKES 4

Toast the bread on both sides until golden brown.
Rub one side of a garlic clove on one side of each piece of bread. Next, rub the bread with the cut sides of the halved tomatoes, pressing the tomato flesh into the toasted bread. Drizzle the bread with oil, then sprinkle with salt.

Spread mayonnaise and/or goat cheese over the tomato- and garlic-rubbed bread. Add arugula/rocket, if using, and the sliced tomatoes to four pieces of the bread. Cover the tomato slices with onions and sprinkle with salt and pepper. Top with the remaining slices of toasted bread, and cut each sandwich diagonally in two.

Serve with Zelda's lemonade (see below).

Zelda's Lemonade

1¾ cups/350 g sugar

8 cups/1.9 liters water

1½ cups/350 ml freshly squeezed lemon juice

ice, to serve

SERVES 4

Combine the sugar and 1 cup/235 ml of water in a small saucepan over medium heat. Keep at an even heat until the sugar has dissolved into the water. When dissolved, take the pan off the heat and set aside to cool.

To serve, combine the lemon juice, sugar syrup, and remaining water in a large pitcher. Add ice if desired.

French Deviled Egg Salad Sandwiches

During the Jazz Age, a variety of American movie stars, journalists, restaurateurs, and writers were emigrating to France, and exerting an impact on French culture. This sandwich is a product of two worlds colliding.

8 large eggs

1½ tablespoons finely chopped green onion

1½ tablespoons finely chopped parsley

1½ tablespoons low-fat mayonnaise

1½ teaspoons mustard

½ teaspoon freshly chopped thyme

½ teaspoon paprika

¼ teaspoon salt

¼ teaspoon freshly ground black pepper

4 slices of ham

1 baguette, sliced lengthwise, then cut into four equal sandwich pieces, or 4 croissants, sliced

mixed lettuce leaves (optional)

1 tomato, thinly sliced (optional)

SERVES 4

Place the eggs in a large saucepan, cover with water to 1 in/ 2.5 cm above the eggs, then bring just to a boil. Remove from the heat, cover, and let stand for 12 minutes. Drain and rinse the eggs in cold running water until cool.

Peel and chop the eggs and place together in a medium bowl. Add the green onion, parsley, mayonnaise, mustard, thyme, paprika, salt, and black pepper, and stir together.

Place a slice of ham in each section of baguette as the bottom layer of filling in the sandwiches. Spoon the egg mixture evenly on top. Add lettuce leaves and tomato, if using, then cover with the top pieces of bread.

Caviar Sandwiches and Champagne

This sandwich is a fluent combination of caviar, smoked salmon, crème fraîche, chives, and fine French sea salt—served with a glass of Champagne, of course. It's a sandwich that would have been served in any of the Parisian bistros that the Fitzgeralds and Hemingways frequented, modeled after the Champagne and caviar parties the Fitzgeralds attended with their friends.

1 small baguette (see page 79), sliced lengthwise, then cut into four equal sandwich pieces

1 tablespoon chives, very finely chopped

1 cup/215 g crème fraîche

8 oz/225 g smoked salmon

2–3 teaspoons caviar

fleur de sel or coarse sea salt

SERVES 4

Cut the baguette as indicated.

To make the sandwich filling, mix the chives and crème fraîche together. Spread a teaspoon of the mixture on each piece of bread. Add the smoked salmon, followed by a half teaspoon (or desired amount) of caviar. Top with a few sprinkles of salt and cover with the top pieces of bread.

Serve with a glass of the finest Champagne.

Oscar Wilde's Cucumber Finger Sandwiches

Natalie Barney was an American poet and prose writer, famous for her weekly salons at her house in the Latin Quarter of Paris. She gathered together many of the greatest cultural figures of the time—Fitzgerald, Colette, Gertrude Stein, Isadora Duncan, Auguste Rodin, T. S. Eliot, and Peggy Guggenheim, among others. Each week she'd serve tea and cucumber sandwiches, memorializing their notable appearance in Wilde's *The Importance of Being Earnest*.

11½-oz/325-g tub cream cheese, whipped

1 garlic clove, finely chopped (optional)

1 teaspoon chopped fresh dill

2–3 chives, finely chopped

1 large seedless cucumber, peeled and thinly sliced by hand or using a mandolin

1 loaf of sandwich bread, very thinly sliced

salt and freshly ground black pepper

SERVES 12

Place the cream cheese, garlic (if using), dill, and chives into a bowl, mix thoroughly, and add salt and pepper to taste.

Assemble the sandwiches by spreading cream cheese thinly across each slice of bread and evenly covering half the cream cheese-covered slices with rounds of the translucently thin cucumber. Sprinkle a tiny amount of salt on the cucumber and top with the another piece of bread. Cut the crusts off.

Serve with tea and good conversation.

Gertrude Stein's Roast Beef Picnic Sandwich

This sandwich is an homage to Gertrude Stein. She and her partner, Alice B. Toklas took many picnics with friends including Ernest Hemingway, F. Scott Fitzgerald and Pablo Picasso during their time in France. While Toklas was a fan of chicken salad, Stein was partial to a roast, as she explained in her 1914 book *Tender Buttons*: "What is more likely than a roast, nothing really and yet it is never disappointed singularly."

2 tablespoons butter

1 shallot, chopped

1 baguette (see page 79), sliced lengthwise, then cut into four equal sandwich pieces

½ cup/100 g crème fraîche

4 large romaine lettuce leaves

8 slices of roast beef

½ cup/100 g Roquefort cheese, sliced

freshly chopped parsley

salt and freshly ground black pepper

1 teaspoon mustard powder

SERVES 4

Melt the butter in a small pan over medium heat, add the shallot, and cook until caramelized. Set aside.

Spread half the crème fraîche evenly on the bottom halves of the four sandwiches. Place a lettuce leaf on top, followed by two slices of roast beef, then top with shallots, Roquefort, and parsley.

Spread the top pieces of bread with the remaining crème fraîche, sprinkle lightly with salt and pepper, if desired, and a pinch of mustard. Add the top halves of the sandwiches and serve.

Fitzgerald's Riviera

One of the most beautiful things about the French Riviera is that it is timeless. It basks in a beauty that is never-changing, and every summer, many make their way to the warm sand and calm sea and set up camp amongst the palm trees between Monaco and St. Raphael. F. Scott Fitzgerald describes the French coast and the Mediterranean memorably in his 1924 essay *How to Live on Practically Nothing a Year*:

"When your eyes first fall upon the Mediterranean you know at once why it was here that man first stood erect and stretched out his arms toward the sun. It is a blue sea; or rather it is too blue for that hackneyed phrase which has described every muddy pool from pole to pole. It is the fairy blue of Maxfield Parrish's pictures; blue like blue books, blue oil, blue eyes, and in the shadow of the mountains a green belt of land runs along the coast for a hundred miles and makes a playground for the world."

But when the Fitzgeralds set sail across the Atlantic on an ocean liner in 1924, Scott's plan was to embrace the simple life of an artist. Despite having been hailed the "voice of the Lost Generation" after *This Side of Paradise* was published in 1920, Fitzgerald, although successful, could no longer afford the champagne lifestyle to which he and Zelda had grown accustomed. The young family opted to leave a busy social life in New York, where booze and parties distracted Fitzgerald from finishing his third novel, *The Great Gatsby*.

After a spell in Paris, they headed down to the Riviera, on the south-east coast of France. Scott wrote *The Great Gatsby* during the summer and fall in a rented hillside villa at Valescure near St. Raphael. On the Riviera, the Fitzgeralds formed a close friendship with affluent and cultured American expats Gerald and Sara Murphy—two wealthy Americans who, by many accounts, were the reason the Riviera became such a hotspot for notable actors, dancers, and writers. The Murphys were known to throw the best soirées, dinner parties, and beach picnics; they were the kind of couple that everyone wanted to be around. Sara, sweet, pretty, and poised, and Gerald, a genial, funny American both came from money and were very good at spending it. The Murphys' charm and joie de vivre was the inspiration behind the characters of Dick and Nicole Diver in Fitzgerald's novel, *Tender Is the Night*.

The Murphys' main headquarters was their home, the Villa America in Cap d'Antibes, where countless dinner parties where thrown. Before that, the Murphys stayed in the notorious Hôtel du Cap Eden-Roc—a pink seaside hotel known best as the Hôtel des Étrangers in *Tender Is the Night*—and the hotel became almost their own. There they entertained the Count and Countess Étienne de Beaumont, Gertrude

Stein, Pablo Picasso and his first wife
Olga Khokhlova, Ernest Hemingway, and,
of course, the Fitzgeralds.

After a brief return to New York, the Fitzgeralds
found themselves back on the Riviera in 1926.
Gatsby had been published and Fitzgerald was
feted as a success. The couple rented the Villa St
Louis in Juan-les-Pins, a house with a private beach
near the casinos.

Scott and Zelda spent the last of their summers on
the Riviera in the summer of 1929 in a more modest
part of Cannes. The Wall Street Crash had taken
its toll and the emphasis was on frugality rather than
expensive parties.

By the time *Tender Is the Night* was published in
1934, the Fitzgeralds and the Murphys had long
since returned to America. Although the Fitzgeralds
would go on to other things in life together and
separately, nothing would ever take those Riviera
summers away from them. As Sara Murphy later
said: "It was like a great fair, and everybody was
so young."

*Scott and Zelda Fitzgerald with their daughter
Scottie, at Antibes in 1926.*

Sara Murphy's Creamed Corn Risotto with Poached Eggs

Great friends of the Fitzgeralds, the Murphys were educated, elegant, and more so, a breath of fresh air. Although they liked to entertain, they delighted most in small, intimate dinner parties. Of their home in Antibes, the art critic Calvin Tomkins wrote of the delicious food that they served, including the American dish of poached eggs on a bed of creamed corn. This Creamed Corn Risotto is an homage to the Murphys' decadence.

1¾ cups/415 ml chicken broth

2 tablespoons butter

1 small yellow onion, finely chopped

¼ teaspoon salt

1 cup/190 g arborio rice

½ cup/70 g creamed corn

¼ cup/60 g goat cheese

¼ cup/20 g grated Parmesan cheese

4–6 poached eggs, to serve
(see page 68) (optional)

SERVES 4–6

Combine the broth with 1½ cups/350 ml water in a saucepan and heat to a simmer; cover and turn the heat to low.

Melt the butter in a 3-quart/2.8-liter saucepan over medium heat. Add the onion and salt and sauté until the onion is lightly browned. Stir in the rice and cook until the edges of the grains become translucent, about 2–3 minutes.

Add 1½ cups/350 ml of the water/broth mix and bring to a simmer. Cook, stirring occasionally, until the liquid is absorbed.

Continue to cook, stirring in about ½ cup/120 ml of the water/broth every few minutes as each addition is absorbed by the rice. Continue adding liquid until the rice is cooked through but still a bit firm in the center. You may not need to use all the liquid prepared.

Stir in the creamed corn and goat cheese, and then the Parmesan. Season with salt and pepper to taste.

If you wish, serve each portion topped with a poached egg (see page 68).

Cervelats and Mustard Sauce

The cervelat, a type of sausage served in Eastern France, Switzerland, and Germany was a favorite of Hemingway. They even get a mention in his memoir *A Moveable Feast*. Serve a smoked or grilled cervelat alongside Hemingway's favorite mustard sauce with Pommes à l'Huile (see page 80) and a cold draft beer.

olive oil, for frying

1 onion, chopped

1 lb/450 g cervelat sausages

DIJON MUSTARD SAUCE

1 cup/225 g mayonnaise, preferably homemade

1 tablespoon Dijon mustard, or more to taste

SERVES 4

Heat some olive oil in a medium skillet/frying pan over medium heat, add the onion, and cook until caramelized. Remove the onion from the pan and keep warm.

Slash the sausages at intervals to prevent the skin splitting as they cook. Add the sausages to the pan and fry until cooked and browned.

Whisk together the mayonnaise and mustard in a small bowl. Taste, and add additional mustard if desired. Spoon the onion over the cooked sausages and serve with the mustard sauce.

Pot au Feu

Pot au Feu (Pot on the Fire) is a classic French dish that was often served at the luncheons held by expat American novelist Gertrude Stein. Her partner, Alice B. Toklas would readily concoct a Pot au Feu for the likes of novelist and playwright Thornton Wilder, Picasso, and even the legendary chef, James Beard. It is said that Pot au Feu was a dish savored by the Fitzgeralds in Paris at the well-known restaurant Le Select Montparnasse.

1½ lb/680 g beef short ribs, in one piece

1½ lb/680 g beef shank

1½ lb/680 g beef brisket

1 onion, peeled, but left whole and studded with 3 cloves

4 garlic cloves, peeled and crushed

bouquet garni (bay leaf, sprigs of thyme and fresh Italian parsley, tied together with kitchen string)

10 whole peppercorns

1 tablespoon coarse sea salt

4 carrots, left whole

4 parsnips, peeled and cut in thirds, lengthwise

4 turnips, peeled and cut in four crosswise

3 leeks, dark ends removed, cut in 4 crosswise, rinsed and tied together

4–6 celery stalks, cut into 1-in/2.5-cm chunks

8 oz/225 g bone marrow (optional)

SERVES 4

Pour 4 pints/2.25 liters cold water into a large, cast-iron pot. Place the short ribs in the water, place over medium-high heat, and boil for 10 minutes, then reduce the heat and simmer, uncovered, for 1 hour.

Add the remaining meat, the onion, garlic, bouquet garni, peppercorns, and salt to the pot. Bring to a boil, skim any scum from the surface, then reduce the heat and simmer, uncovered, for 2 hours.

Add the carrots, parsnips, turnips, leeks, and celery. Cook slowly for another hour.

If using marrow bones, poach them in slightly salted water for 20 minutes.

Serve the broth separately from the meat and vegetables. Strain the broth through a cheesecloth and serve as hot as possible with a side of homemade mayonnaise (see page 47), Dijon mustard sauce (see page 43), and toasted baguette (see page 79).

Steak Tartare, or Steak à l'Americaine

Steak Tartare is traditional brasserie food, which was probably enjoyed by Fitzgerald and Hemingway during their roadtrip from Lyon to Paris.

14 oz/400 g trimmed center-cut beef tenderloin

1½ tablespoons Dijon mustard

2 egg yolks

¼ cup/60 ml canola/rapeseed oil

6 tablespoons salt-packed capers, rinsed, drained, and finely chopped

2 tablespoons finely chopped fresh parsley

1½ tablespoons Worcestershire sauce

¼ teaspoon hot sauce, such as Tabasco

4 cornichons, finely chopped

1 small yellow onion, finely chopped

kosher salt and freshly ground black pepper

sliced pears, to serve

mixed salad greens, to serve

SERVES 4

Place the beef in the freezer for about 30 minutes, to firm up—this will make it easier to chop finely.

Meanwhile, whisk the mustard and egg yolks in a large bowl; whisking constantly, slowly pour in the oil to create a mayonnaise. Add the capers, parsley, Worcestershire sauce, hot sauce, cornichons, and onion, and season with salt and pepper. Refrigerate until ready to use.

Remove the beef from the freezer and cut into ¼-in/5-mm cubes. Transfer the beef to the bowl of mayonnaise and stir to combine. Keep the beef mixture chilled until ready to serve.

To serve, divide the beef mixture into four equal portions, shape each into an oval disk, and place on individual serving plates. Serve immediately with some sliced pears and a handful of mixed salad greens.

Chapter Three
Hors d'Oeuvres

Smoked Salmon Mousse

French Shrimp Cocktail

Salmon Tartare

Escargots

Harlequin Salad

Pork Rillettes and Apple Jelly

Smoked Salmon Mousse

In Parisian cafés and restaurants, many artists, writers, and composers would gather for a drink after their working day. Salmon mousse was often served during cocktail hour and was a favorite of many of the happy-hour patrons. This way of serving makes it a perfect canapé. It's crunchy, delicious, and a little bit luxurious.

4 oz/120 g smoked salmon

2 tablespoons heavy/double cream

8-oz/225g package cream cheese, softened

freshly squeezed juice of ½ lemon

1 tablespoon fresh dill, finely chopped, plus a few sprigs for decoration

1 oz/25 g salmon roe

salt and freshly ground black pepper

1 large cucumber, sliced, to serve

SERVES 4

Place the smoked salmon in a blender or food processor, and blend until smooth. Mix in the cream, cream cheese, lemon juice, finely chopped dill, salt, and pepper. Blend to the desired consistency.

Pipe the salmon mousse onto thick slices of cucumber and garnish with salmon roe and the remaining sprigs of dill.

French Shrimp Cocktail

Not your typical modern shrimp cocktail recipe, here small shrimp (prawns) are used and mixed with the cocktail sauce. Spoon into a bowl lined with lettuce and serve very chilled. This is the sort of recipe that the Fitzgeralds, the Murphys, and any of the American expats in 1920s Paris might have enjoyed as an appetizer before lunch.

4 tablespoons mayonnaise

2 teaspoons cream sherry

2 tablespoons tomato purée

1–2 tablespoons freshly squeezed
lemon juice

20 small shrimp/prawns, peeled

1 head of lettuce

a little paprika

SERVES 4

Mix together the mayonnaise, sherry, the tomato purée, and the lemon juice in a bowl. Add the shrimp/prawns and a little more tomato purée, if necessary, to give a light pink color.

Shred the lettuce and arrange in glass dishes. Spoon the shrimp mixture on top. Take a small pinch of paprika with your fingers and sprinkle over each shrimp cocktail, then serve.

Salmon Tartare

Much of the cuisine in the French Riviera is dependent on seasonal fruits and vegetables, but also its climate and geography, so it's no surprise that seafood and fish feature heavily. Dishes such as Lobster Salad (see page 78) and Bouillabaisse (see page 88) have remained popular for generations. Salmon Tartare is another popular local delicacy and is quick and easy to prepare. It's a dish that Sara Murphy or Nicole Diver would have enjoyed immensely.

8 oz/225 g center-cut salmon fillet, skin and pin bones removed, cut into ¼-in/5-mm dice

1 tablespoon finely chopped shallots

1 tablespoon finely chopped fresh chives, plus extra to garnish

1 tablespoon finely chopped fresh flat-leaf parsley

1½ teaspoons freshly squeezed lemon juice

1 tablespoon extra-virgin olive oil, plus extra for drizzling

¾ teaspoon kosher or sea salt

pinch or two of freshly ground white pepper

1 English cucumber

fleur de sel or coarse sea salt, to serve

1 baguette (see page 79)

SERVES 4

Place the salmon in a medium bowl. Gently fold in the shallots, chives, parsley, and lemon juice. Stir in the olive oil and add the salt and pepper. Cover and refrigerate for at least 30 minutes, or up to 8 hours. Remove from the fridge 20 minutes before serving.

Cut the cucumber in half crosswise. Cut each half into long, paper-thin ribbons. Set aside on a plate, covered, until ready to serve.

To assemble, using large salad or dinner plates, scatter several long slices of cucumber around each plate in a random, artful way. Leave the center of each plate open. Spoon even amounts of salmon tartare into a mound in the center of each plate. Drizzle olive oil over the cucumber slices, garnish with chives, and sprinkle with a little salt. Serve immediately with a thinly sliced baguette.

Escargots

Escargot (snails) were becoming a delicacy in Paris during the Jazz Age.
In a well-known restaurant named l'Escargot Montorgueil, with its signature
giant golden snail on the facade, diners from all over the world came
to eat snails. You should try them—you will not be disappointed!

36 wild snails, out of their shells (preferably from Burgundy)

4 tablespoons butter

5 oz/140 g shallots, finely chopped

1 head of garlic, cloves finely chopped

bunch of flat-leaf parsley, finely chopped

6 tablespoons coarse breadcrumbs

Garlic butter

1 lb/450 g butter, at room temperature

bunch of flat-leaf Italian parsley, stems discarded, leaves chopped

¼ bunch of tarragon, leaves chopped

½ head of garlic, cloves chopped

1 tablespoon fine sea salt

2 teaspoons freshly ground black pepper

Special equipment: 6 snail gratin dishes

Serves 6

Rinse the snails. Melt the butter in a sauté pan over low heat. Add the snails, shallot, and garlic and slowly sauté for 10 minutes. Season to taste and finish by adding the parsley. Set aside and let it cool.

Preheat the oven to 350°F (175°C) Gas 4.

To prepare the butter, mix the ingredients in a blender until very smooth. Season to taste.

To assemble, place 1 snail in each hole of the gratin dishes and cover up to the brim with garlic butter. Sprinkle breadcrumbs over each snail. Bake in the preheated oven for 6–8 minutes until the butter is slightly bubbling.

For escargots with Roquefort, serve with 2 oz/50 g of Roquefort cheese on the side. For escargots with curry, add 1 tablespoon of mild curry powder to the melted butter in the sauté pan.

You can also cook the snails in their shells, which are often supplied with the canned snails. Put a snail in each shell, and fill with plenty of garlic butter, then breadcrumbs. Place 1 shell in each hole in the gratin dish. Bake in the oven, as above.

Harlequin Salad

"At least once a fortnight a corps of caterers came down with several hundred feet of canvas and enough colored lights to make a Christmas tree of Gatsby's enormous garden. On buffet tables, garnished with glistening hors-d'oeuvre, spiced baked hams crowded against salads of harlequin designs and pastry pigs and turkeys bewitched to a dark gold. In the main hall a bar with a real brass rail was set up, and stocked with gins and liquors and with cordials so long forgotten that most of his female guests were too young to know one from another." (*The Great Gatsby*)

FRENCH LENTIL SALAD

²/₃ cup/125 g Puy or French lentils
(equivalent to 1½ cups when cooked)

1 bay leaf

2 ears fresh sweetcorn

2 firm red tomatoes, finely chopped

2 green onions, green and
white parts, finely chopped

3 tablespoons freshly chopped parsley

3 tablespoons freshly chopped
or torn basil

⅓ cup/40 g Kalamata olives,
pitted and finely chopped

⅓ cup goat cheese, crumbled

DRESSING

2 tablespoons olive oil

1 teaspoon red wine vinegar

freshly squeezed juice of 1 lime
(about 2 tablespoons)

1 teaspoon sea salt

¼ teaspoon cayenne pepper

freshly ground black pepper

Rinse the lentils under cold running water, then place in a bowl, cover generously with water, and soak for 2 hours. Drain and rinse, then transfer to a small saucepan and cover with several inches of fresh water. Add the bay leaf and bring to a boil. Reduce the heat to low, cover, and simmer for 15–20 minutes or until the lentils are tender. Drain and discard the bay leaf. Set aside to cool.

Meanwhile, preheat the oven to 400°F (200°C) Gas 6. Roast the ears of corn in their husks for 30 minutes or until tender. Alternatively, broil/grill the corn in their husks on a barbecue for about 15 minutes, turning frequently. Set aside to cool, then pare the kernels from the ears.

Place the lentils, corn, tomatoes, green onions, parsley, and basil in a large mixing bowl. Whisk together the dressing ingredients and toss about half of the dressing with the salad. Scatter the olives and goat cheese over the top and lightly toss with the remaining dressing. Serve at room temperature. If preparing ahead of time, reserve the parsley and basil and mix in just before serving.

Beet Salad

10 oz/285 g peas, cooked

15 oz/425 g roasted beets/beetroot, diced

½ onion, finely chopped

½ cup/115 g mayonnaise

8–10 asparagus spears, steamed

Serves 4

To make the beet salad, in a medium bowl, mix together the peas, beets, onion, and mayonnaise. Refrigerate for about 30 minutes until cold, before serving.

To assemble, on a long rectangular serving dish, arrange spears in a crisscross pattern to create a harlequin design with diamond shapes in the middle and triangles framing the sides. Fill in the diamonds with beet salad and the triangles with lentil salad.

The Jazz Age

For most of us there are a few things that epitomize the 1920s: the Charleston, flappers, bobbed hair, short skirts, and *The Great Gatsby* all spring to mind. Those romantics among us also tend to fondly reference 1920s' Paris, a unique place and time that gave a home to the creators of some of the greatest works of art, literature, and music of the twentieth century.

Following the creatives to Paris were the socialites, the movie stars, and finally the musicians. George Antheil was considered one of the greats of his generation. At age 21, he was already a musical prodigy when he sailed to France hoping to make his mark as a pianist. Antheil was a remarkable musician who would later go on to be a journalist and novelist.

Aaron Copland studied under Nadia Boulanger, a famous teacher to a bevy of musicians from Virgil Thomson to Quincy Jones. In addition to being a mentor, Boulanger was a pianist and organist. Copland wrote his Organ Symphony under her direction in 1924.

Also on the scene were two of America's most popular music composers, George Gershwin and Cole Porter. Already a big deal in the United States, they too were soon mixing with Picasso, Stein, Charlie Chaplin, and others. Before long, France was awash with the music of Cole Porter and George and Ira Gershwin. In return, Gershwin composed his jazz-influenced "tone poem" *An American in Paris*, inspired by the sights and sounds of his adopted city, and incorporating the blues music of his homeland.

Cole Porter not only wrote some of the most popular songs of the Jazz Age culture, but in 1923 he wrote a jazz-based short ballet with Fitzgerald's friend Gerald Murphy, and later enjoyed his first Broadway success with a musical entitled *Paris*.

And of course, there was jazz itself. Commonly agreed to have originated in the city of New Orleans in the USA, itself once a French colony, jazz music was adopted with enthusiasm by Parisians in the 1920s, especially in the clubs and bars of Montparnasse.

The Jazz Age was a time when music was taking over in an intoxicating fashion. Jazz was in vogue and the young ladies and gentleman of the world were staying out late, drinking, and rebelling against the more traditional way they had been raised. And who could blame them—when one listens to Duke Ellington, George Gershwin, and various other jazz greats, it's easy to see why music held so much "sway" over this young generation.

Escaping civil rights inequalities back home, many African-American musicians and artistes arrived in Paris, following the trail set by Josephine Baker, an

Josephine Baker (center) dining at the restaurant Chez Josephine in around 1928, with Georges Simenon and his wife.

African-American, who performed nightly to packed audiences in smoky cabarets. Baker had a unique voice and audacious yet graceful stage presence. She was able to live and work in a more tolerant environment in Paris—France was years ahead of other countries in its openness to art, no matter the skin color of the person creating it. Her success paved the way for other African-Americans artistes, including jazz musicians, to come to Paris to live and to perform.

With many creative expats flooding into the Montparnasse district of Paris, it soon became a center for the arts. Its many galleries, cafés, bars, and restaurants were places for lonely Americans and the French to mingle. Paris was a city of new ideas, new philosophies, and new outlooks. It suited those who, in Fitzgerald's words, were "...a generation, grown up to find all wars fought, all Gods dead and all faith in mankind shaken."

Pork Rillettes
and Apple Jelly

It's fitting to think that this might be a Fitzgerald favorite, as it is essentially the French version of pulled pork, a popular dish in the American south. The Fitzgeralds adored a party and when they were up, they were up. For an appetizer that acts as a good symbol of Zelda Fitzgerald's heritage—a little bit country, a little bit couture—this recipe for Pork Rillettes is sure to be one you'll fancy. Pair with a glass of Champagne, a baguette, and some apple jelly.

Pork Rillettes

1 lb/450 g pork belly,
coarsely chopped

1 lb/450 g boneless pork shoulder,
coarsely chopped

¼ teaspoon mustard seeds

½ teaspoon freshly ground
black pepper

2 teaspoons *fleur de sel* or coarse salt

5 garlic cloves, crushed

2 bay leaves

1 cup/235 ml Champagne

Baguette, to serve (see page 79)

Dijon mustard sauce (see page 43)
(optional)

pickles (optional)

SERVES 4

Place the pork belly and shoulder in a large pot. Add the mustard seeds, pepper, salt, garlic and one of the bay leaves and mix together. Pour in the Champagne and, over medium-high heat, bring the mixture to a boil. Once boiling, turn the heat down and bring to a slow simmer. Let simmer for 30 minutes, periodically skimming any foam. Add 1 cup/235 ml water, return to a very slow simmer, cover, and cook for 2½ hours, stirring once or twice.

After the pork mixture has simmered, uncover it and increase the heat to medium. Let cook for a further 30 minutes until the liquid is all fat—you don't want any water. Season to taste. Set aside for at least 1 hour to cool. Remove the bay leaf.

Either gently pulse the mixture a few times in a food processor or use two forks and/or your fingers to mash the mixture. Transfer to a clean jar with a lid that clamps and/or does not let in any air bubbles. Top with the other bay leaf, secure the jar's lid, and place in the fridge for at least 4 hours or, preferably, overnight. Let it come to room temperature about 30 minutes before serving.

Serve with sliced baguette, apple jelly, and Dijon mustard sauce and pickles, if liked.

Apple Jelly

peel and cores from 8–10 apples (ideally a mixture of mostly sweet dessert apples)

about 3 cups/700 ml water

splash of freshly squeezed lemon juice

½ box/20 g dry pectin

4½ cups/900 g sugar

pinch of salt

MAKES 2–3 JARS, DEPENDING ON JAR SIZE (RECIPE CAN BE DOUBLED)

Place the apple peel and cores in a pan with the water and cook over low heat for 15 minutes.

Strain the cores and peels through a prepared cheesecloth or jelly bag into a large bowl. Measure the strained juice and add enough water to obtain 3½ cups/840 ml of liquid, then pour the liquid into a clean pan.

Whisk the pectin into the liquid. Place over a high heat and bring to a rapid boil. Add the sugar and salt, then boil fiercely for 1 minute.

Pour into sterilized jars, leaving ⅛ in/3 mm of space at the top of each jar. Seal in a canner or refrigerate for up to 2 weeks.

Chapter Four
Soups and Salads

French Onion Soup and Salade Lyonnaise

James Joyce's Beef Tea

Scott's Tomato Soup

Vichysoisse

Salade Niçoise

French Lobster Salad

French Baguette

Pommes à l'Huile

Chicken Salad Stuffed Tomatoes

French Onion Soup and Salade Lyonnaise

La Rotonde, Harry's, Le Dôme, Café de Flore, and other traditional French bistros were regular haunts of Fitzgerald, T. S. Eliot, and Picasso—especially Fitzgerald. Perfect for gray Paris days, onion soup was as much a café favorite back in the 1920s as it is today. Add a Salade Lyonnaise for a perfect bistro duo.

French Onion Soup

6 tablespoons unsalted butter

1 tablespoon olive oil

3 lb/1.3 kg Vidalia (or sweet) onions (about 6 medium), peeled, halved lengthwise, and thinly sliced (with a mandolin or by hand)

1 teaspoon *fleur de sel* or coarse sea salt

½ teaspoon freshly ground black pepper

½ teaspoon brown sugar

10 sprigs of fresh thyme

2 bay leaves

1½ cups/350 ml dry white wine

6 cups/1.4 liters beef broth (see recipe for Beef Tea page 71, or use store-bought)

1 baguette (see page 79)

1 garlic clove, cut in half lengthwise

2 teaspoons sherry (optional)

½ cup/50 g Gruyère cheese, grated

½ cup/50 g Swiss cheese, grated

Special equipment: 4 ramekins and cheesecloth/kitchen twine

SERVES 4

Melt 4 tablespoons of the butter in a large pot over medium heat. Add the oil and onions and cook until the onions have softened, stirring occasionally, about 15 minutes. Add the salt, pepper, and brown sugar; continue to cook, stirring occasionally, until the onions are deep golden brown and caramelized, reducing the heat slightly if they start to brown too quickly, 35–45 minutes.

Add the wine to deglaze the pan and raise the heat to high. Cook until almost all the liquid has evaporated, about 10 minutes.

Tie the thyme and bay leaves into a bundle with twine or enclose in a cheesecloth/muslin bundle. Add to the onions. Pour in the beef broth. Bring to a boil, then reduce to a simmer and cook, uncovered, until the broth is thickened and flavorful, 25–30 minutes. Remove from the heat, discard the herbs, and whisk in the remaining 2 tablespoons of butter. Taste and adjust the seasoning.

Preheat the broiler/grill.

Cut two ½-in/1-cm baguette slices for every serving of soup. Place the baguette slices on a baking sheet or cookie sheet and toast until crisp and dry but not browned, about 1 minute each side. Rub one side of each toast with the garlic clove and set aside.

Place the ramekins on a rimmed baking sheet, add ½ teaspoon of sherry to the bottom of each, then ladle the soup on top. Top each serving of soup with two garlic-rubbed toasts. Divide the cheese among the servings, covering the bread and some of the soup. Carefully transfer the baking sheet to the broiler/grill until the cheese is melted and bubbling, about 5 minutes. Serve straight away.

Salade Lyonnaise

8 slices of bacon

4 slices of day-old French bread

1½ tablespoons butter, melted

4 tablespoons olive oil

4 tablespoons white wine vinegar

2 teaspoons Dijon mustard sauce
(see page 43)

4 eggs

1 teaspoon vinegar (optional)

1 head of frisée lettuce, torn into
bite-sized pieces

1 shallot, chopped

salt and freshly ground black pepper

Serves 4

Cook the bacon in a skillet/frying pan over medium heat until crisp, about 10 minutes. Remove from the heat and drain the pan of excess fat. Once the bacon is cool, chop into ½-in/1-cm pieces. Set aside.

Cut the French bread into cubes. Melt the butter in the same skillet/frying pan, then add the bread and toast over medium heat. Do not stir the bread unless to turn to a different side once one side is browned. Set aside.

In a medium-large jar, mix the olive oil, vinegar, mustard sauce, and some salt and pepper by giving it a good shake.

To poach the eggs, fill a saucepan about two-thirds full with water and bring to a boil. Turn the heat down and let the water return to a high simmer—you should see bubbles coming up to the surface, but it won't be rolling. Crack an egg into a small measuring cup, preferably one with a long handle as this will help you ease the egg into the water. If you wish, add a teaspoon of vinegar to the water—this helps the egg keep its shape. Ease the egg into the water, using the measuring cup to tip it out once it is in the water. Cook for about 4 minutes. Remove the egg from the water with a slotted spoon and place on a plate. Pat dry very delicately with paper towel. (I poach these one at a time because they are very delicate.)

Layer the frisée, chopped bacon, chopped shallot, and croutons on four salad plates. Pour the dressing over the salad and toss lightly. Top each plate with a poached egg.

James Joyce's Beef Tea

Beef tea, also known as beef broth, is a thick, rich stock that was popular with men and women of Irish descent. In Ireland it was used to feed invalids, but also to warm one up on a cold day. James Joyce was not only a fan of it in everyday life, usually enjoying a cup daily, but also mentioned it in many of the stories that he wrote in Paris.

4 lb/1.8 kg beef short rib bones

3 carrots, cut roughly into chunks

3 celery stalks, cut into chunks

2 Vidalia (or sweet) onions, quartered

½ cup/120 ml warm water

3 bay leaves

5 garlic cloves

8–10 whole peppercorns

3 sprigs of fresh parsley

1 teaspoon each dried thyme, marjoram, rosemary, and oregano

about 3 quarts/2.8 liters cold water

MAKES 2 QUARTS/1.9 LITERS

Preheat the oven to 450°F (230°C) Gas 8.

Place the bones in a large roasting pan. Roast, uncovered, for 30 minutes. Add the carrots, celery, and onions to the pan and roast for another 30 minutes. Remove from the oven and drain the fat.

Using a slotted spoon, transfer the bones and vegetables to a large pot. Add the warm water to roasting pan; stir to deglaze and loosen the browned bits from pan. Transfer the pan juices to the pot of bones and vegetables. Add the seasonings and enough cold water just to cover.

Slowly bring to a boil over medium heat, about 30 minutes. Reduce the heat and simmer, uncovered, for 4–5 hours, skimming the surface as foam rises. If necessary, add more hot water during the first 2 hours to keep the ingredients covered.

Remove the bones and set the broth aside until cool enough to handle. Strain the broth through a cheesecloth-lined colander or strainer, discarding the vegetables and seasonings. If using immediately, skim the fat. Alternatively, cool, then refrigerate for 8 hours or overnight and then remove the fat from the surface. Broth can be covered and refrigerated for up to 3 days or frozen for 4–6 months.

Scott's Tomato Soup

The Fitzgeralds' relationship was fueled by passion. Passion and lots of gin.
The two of them were often the life and soul of the party, but they were notorious
tricksters, and they made a few enemies with their antics. One of their more
infamous moments occurred at a party thrown by Lois Moran, a 17-year old movie
star that Scott had met at a luncheon. Zelda and Scott had been encountering a few
marital bumps and before long, Scott developed a crush on Lois. At the party, the
couple showed up the worse for wear. Scott went around collecting watches
and jewelry from guests, and then boiled them all up in a pot of tomato soup.
This recipe is an homage to that tomato soup. Jewelry-inclusion optional.

¾ teaspoon dried basil

½ teaspoon fennel seeds

½ teaspoon dried oregano

½ teaspoon dried thyme

good-tasting extra-virgin olive oil

3 onions, diced

3 large garlic cloves, finely chopped

⅓ cup/125 g tomato paste

⅓ cup/90 ml dry vermouth

2 lb/900g vine tomatoes, peeled,
seeded and chopped, or a 28-oz/
790g can whole tomatoes with their
juice, crushed

2 x 14-oz/395g cans vegetable broth

⅛ teaspoon cinnamon, or to taste

4 oz/100 g fresh goat cheese,
crumbled

salt and freshly ground black pepper

Serves 4

Using a food processor or coffee grinder, combine the herbs and
pulse, or pound together using a mortar and pestle. Set aside.

Cover the bottom of a large pot with the olive oil and place
over medium-high heat. Stir in the onions, season with salt and
pepper, and cook for 5–6 minutes until golden brown, stirring
often. Add the herbs and garlic. Continue cooking for about 30
seconds until their aromas are released.

Stir in the tomato paste until there are no lumps, then add the
vermouth and tomatoes. Combine and boil for 2 minutes. Pour in
the broth and ⅔ cup/150 ml water and mix well to combine.
Adjust the heat to a steady simmer, cover with a lid, and cook for
20 minutes. Add the cinnamon, then taste the soup for seasoning.

Ladle the soup into bowls and top with the crumbled goat cheese.

Vichyssoise

Although its origins are contested, this classic soup is thought to have been created in New York in 1912 by a French chef named Louis Diat, of the Ritz Carlton. He made it by adapting an existing French recipe, and by the 1920s it was being served in Paris—but as an American dish. It's a thick, rich soup made with chicken stock, leeks, onion, and potato, and it was a favorite of many expats. This soup is delicious either hot or cold.

2 garlic cloves, smashed and finely chopped

2 leeks, chopped

1 onion, chopped

3 tablespoons unsalted butter

4–6 oz/115–170 g peeled and thinly sliced potato (about 1 medium potato)

2⅓ cups/560 ml chicken or veal stock, or duck broth (see page 104)

1⅛ cups/265 ml heavy/double cream

salt and freshly ground black pepper

SERVES 4

In a medium saucepan over medium heat, gently sweat the garlic, leeks, and onion in the butter until soft, about 5–6 minutes.

Add the potatoes and stock to the saucepan, and season to taste (but do not overdo the salt and pepper). Bring to a boil, then simmer very gently for 30 minutes.

Transfer to a blender or food processor and purée until very smooth. Let cool. Gently stir in the cream before serving either warm or cold.

Salade Niçoise

In the French Riviera, Salade Niçoise is a really big deal. So big, in fact, that there is a committee in Nice dedicated to preserving its authenticity and its history. This Salade Niçoise is an authentic version, such as would have been served at places like the Hotel du Cap-Eden-Roc, which was host to many famous dignitaries, debutantes, and celebrities during the 1920s, the Fitzgeralds included.

1 lb/450 g red-skinned potatoes, cut into ⅓-in/5-mm slices

fleur de sel or coarse sea salt

2 tablespoons dry white wine

10 oz/285 g thin green beans, trimmed

4 large eggs

¼ cup/60 ml white wine vinegar

½ shallot, finely chopped

2 tablespoons Dijon mustard

1½ tablespoons freshly chopped thyme

¾ cup/175 ml extra-virgin olive oil

8 cherry tomatoes, halved

1 head of Boston lettuce, leaves separated

6 radishes, trimmed and quartered

2 x 5½-oz/155-g cans Italian or Spanish tuna in olive oil, drained

½ cup/50 g pitted Niçoise olives

¼ cup/50 g anchovies (optional)

freshly ground black pepper

SERVES 4

Place the potatoes in a saucepan, cover with cold water, and season with salt, then bring to a simmer over medium heat. Cook for about 5 minutes or until the potatoes are tender. Remove from the heat and transfer the potatoes and their cooking water to a medium bowl. Slowly pour the wine over them and let cool in the water-wine. Reserve the saucepan for later use.

Meanwhile, blanche the green beans by bringing a saucepan of salted water to a boil and set aside a water bath filled with ice. Add the beans to the boiling water for 30 seconds, then remove from the water and immediately drop into the ice bath. Drain, and set the beans aside.

Place the eggs in the reserved saucepan and cover with cold water by about 1 in/2.5 cm. Bring to a simmer over medium-high heat, then cover, remove from the heat, and let stand for 10–12 minutes. Drain, then run under cold water to cool. Peel under cold running water.

Whisk together the vinegar, shallot, mustard, thyme, 1/2 teaspoon salt, and pepper to taste in a bowl. Whisk in the olive oil slowly and combine until emulsified.

Toss the tomatoes in a small bowl with salt and pepper to taste. Add about 4 tablespoons of the dressing to the potatoes and toss. Quarter the hard-boiled eggs.

Divide the lettuce among four plates. Arrange the potatoes, radishes, eggs, and tuna on top. Pour any juices from the tomatoes into the dressing, then add the tomatoes to the plates. Drizzle with the dressing and top with the olives. If using anchovies, arrange them on top of the salad.

French Lobster Salad

In *Tender Is the Night*, Fitzgerald describes the Carlton Hotel in Cannes: "The hotel and its bright tan prayer rug of a beach were one." The Carlton Hotel is still one of the most beautiful settings for a meal in the Côte d'Azur, and this Lobster Salad is the kind of dish you might still find on the menu at the legendary hotel restaurant that's been feeding the well-heeled for decades.

1 cooked lobster, about 1 lb/450 g

2 tablespoons Champagne vinegar

1½ teaspoons Dijon mustard
(see page 98)

1½ tablespoons freshly chopped
tarragon

5 tablespoons extra-virgin olive oil

2 heads of butter lettuce,
torn into large pieces

1 orange or tangerine, peeled
and segmented

1 ruby red grapefruit, peeled
and segmented

1 tablespoon freshly chopped chives

salt and freshly ground black pepper

SERVES 4

Cut the cooked lobster meat into ½-in/1-cm pieces.

In a small bowl, whisk together the vinegar, mustard, half the tarragon, salt, and pepper. Add the olive oil in a slow, steady stream, whisking constantly until smooth and blended.

In a large bowl, combine the lettuce with about 2 tablespoons of the vinaigrette and gently toss to coat the lettuce evenly. Transfer the lettuce to a chilled platter.

In the same bowl, combine the lobster meat with about 1 tablespoon of the vinaigrette and gently toss to coat the lobster evenly. Scatter the lobster over the lettuce and garnish with the orange and grapefruit segments. Sprinkle with the chives and remaining tarragon and serve immediately.

French Baguette

Believe it or not, the baguette did not make its first appearance in French cuisine until 1920. A law was passed that prevented many food service workers from starting work before 4am. This made it difficult for bakers to have fresh bread ready in time for breakfast. The solution was to shape the dough into long, thin *baguettes* (from the Latin *baculum*, or "stick") that cooked at a faster rate.

2 cups/473 ml warm water (110°F /43°C)

1 teaspoon sugar

3¼ teaspoons active dry yeast

5–5½ cups/650–700 g all-purpose/plain flour, plus extra for dusting

2½ teaspoons salt

1 egg white, lightly beaten with a pinch of salt

MAKES 2 LOAVES

In a small bowl, combine the warm water and sugar, stirring until the sugar dissolves. Add the yeast and stir gently to mix. Let stand until foamy, about 5 minutes.

In the bowl of an electric mixer fitted with the dough hook, combine 4 cups/550 g of the flour and the salt. Beat on low speed just until combined. Slowly add the yeast mixture and beat just until incorporated, about 1 minute. Increase the speed to medium and beat for 10 minutes, adding more flour, about ¼ cup/40 g at a time, until the dough is elastic and pulls away from the sides of the bowl.

Turn the dough out onto a lightly floured surface and knead for 1 minute. Form into a ball and dust lightly with flour. Sprinkle a little flour into a large bowl and transfer the dough to the bowl. Cover with plastic wrap/clingfilm and let rise in a warm place until doubled in size (45–60 minutes).

Turn the dough out onto a lightly floured surface. Punch down the dough and knead for a few seconds. Form the dough into a ball and return to the bowl again. Cover the bowl with plastic wrap/clingfilm and let rise in a warm place until doubled in size (20–30 minutes).

Turn the dough out onto a lightly floured surface and punch down. Cut the dough into two equal pieces and shape each into a ball. Let rest for 5 minutes.

Line a baking sheet with a clean dish towel (a large flour sack works well) and sprinkle with a little flour. Roll each ball into a log with tapered ends, about the length of the baking sheet, and place on the towel. Cover with the overhanging edges of the towel and let rise in a warm place for 20 minutes.

Preheat the oven to 425°F (220°C) Gas 7. Position an oven rack in the lowest position in the oven, and place a baking pan one-third full of boiling water on the rack.

Gently lift the towel holding the loaves off of the baking sheet, taking care not to let the loaves touch each other and set on a work surface. Spray the sheet with non-stick cooking spray, and, using the towel as a guide, gently flip each loaf onto the baking sheet. Brush off any excess flour.

Using a sharp knife, make 3–5 diagonal slashes in the loaves about ¼ in/5 mm deep. Brush with the beaten egg white mixture. Bake on the center rack until the bread is golden brown and sounds hollow when tapped, 30–35 minutes. Transfer the sheet to a wire rack and cool the loaves to room temperature.

Pommes à l'Huile

Essentially a fresh, French potato salad, this dish was a favorite of Hemingway, who described its fundamentals of firm potatoes, delicious olive oil, and freshly-ground black pepper in his memoir *A Moveable Feast*. This dish is best served with a baguette (see page 79) and some Cervelats (see page 42), mustard sauce, or Dijon mustard (see page 98) and a cold draft beer.

3 lb/1.3 kg new potatoes, scrubbed clean, skin on

1 cup/235 ml extra-virgin olive oil, plus extra 4 tablespoons for the dressing

6 tablespoons good-quality white wine vinegar

4 tablespoons dry white wine

2 teaspoons kosher salt or *fleur de sel*

4 small shallots, finely chopped

3–4 tablespoons finely chopped fresh parsley

1 tablespoon very finely chopped fresh thyme, or to taste

3 tablespoons finely chopped fresh chives

freshly ground black pepper

SERVES 4

Steam the unpeeled potatoes on for 20 minutes, or until tender when pricked with a fork. Drain and let cool.

Meanwhile, whisk together 1 cup olive oil, 4 tablespoons of the vinegar, the wine, and salt.

Peel the potatoes and slice ½ in/1 cm thick. Toss with the vinaigrette and set aside for about 30 minutes to allow the potatoes to absorb the liquid.

In a small bowl, combine the remaining vinegar, olive oil shallots, parsley, thyme, and chives. Add pepper to taste.

Before serving the potatoes, quickly toss with the fresh herbed vinaigrette.

Chicken Salad Stuffed Tomatoes

In *The Beautiful and Damned*, published in 1922, Gloria Gilbert is a dinner host's worst nightmare. The character is widely believed to have been influenced by Fitzgerald's wife, Zelda. On a visit to Los Angeles, as they sit down to dine, Gloria announces that she will refuse to stray from her already restrictive diet of tomatoes and celery. As the waiter sets down a plate of tomatoes stuffed with chicken salad, Gloria becomes infuriated. And for good reason: her tomatoes always come stuffed with celery. Unfortunately for Gloria, her intransigence is matched by that of the waiter, who equally enjoys upholding his own traditions:
"We always serve it that way, madame.'"
This doesn't improve the situation, so Antony tries another tack:
"Why don't you try to eat it? It can't be as bad as you think."
And so she does, tentatively at first, but then "in another moment she was eating".

1 lb/450 g poached chicken breast, chopped into small chunks

1 cup/130 g chopped celery

4 scallions/spring onions, chopped

1 cup/225 g mayonnaise

½ teaspoon celery salt

½ cup/40 g slivered/flaked almonds

8–10 tomatoes, cored, or 4 avocados, halved and stones removed

SERVES 4

Stir together the chicken, celery, scallions/spring onions, mayonnaise, celery salt, and almonds until well combined.

Scoop the mixture into cored tomatoes or avocados, and serve cold.

Cafés

A Home from Home

The romance of Parisian café culture in the 1920s is enchanting, from rivalries stirred over coffee and conversation to penniless authors seeking a warm place to work. A quick bite or a lingering daytime coffee could easily slip into early evening cocktails, and cafés were a good place in which to unwind after a long day of writing novels, painting, or merely struggling to survive in a city like Paris on an artist's budget.

Many of those in the "Lost Generation"—young survivors of World War One—frequented the Parisian cafés as a way to meet like-minded artists, but also perhaps a wealthy expat or two. In such surroundings, Fitzgerald received a lot of dinner party invitations and gave out many compliments to other writers who ran within the same circles. In his later years James Joyce, although considered accomplished by his peers, was penniless. A cup of tea could be made to last for hours, while he sat and wrote in the warmth and comfort of the café.

Actors, dancers, painters, and musicians served as wonderful nighttime company for Scott and Zelda, but these friends were less likely to be found at work in the cafés—for obvious reasons as for most, their craft required much more than a pad of paper and a pen.

During the Jazz Age, La Rotonde was the first port of call for Americans in Paris—a café that welcomed Bohemians and newly rooted Parisians with open arms. It played host to a variety of well-

known writers, including Gertrude Stein, T.S. Eliot, and Scott Fitzgerald. The café was even written about by Ernest Hemingway in his 1926 novel *The Sun Also Rises*. Years later, La Rotonde is still a place where artists and travelers head to seek inspiration and bask in its associations. If you didn't bump into Fitzgerald at La Rotonde, you might well find him at Le Dôme Café on the Boulevard du Montparnasse. Later, Le Select and Le Couple would emerge as competitors to La Rotonde—all serving as magnets for European and American artists alike.

One of the most notorious hangouts for the likes of not only Fitzgerald, but other highly regarded writers, poets, and artists, such as French poet Arthur Rimbaud, French writer and philosopher Simone de Beauvoir, and Pablo Picasso, is the much-celebrated Les Deux Magots, one of the oldest cafés in Paris. One of their best-loved drinks is hot chocolate, a delicacy James Joyce surely enjoyed when he could afford it. Les Deux Magots is still open today and is largely frequented by tourists hoping to walk in the shoes of those renowned erstwhile customers. It is still a good place to cozy up with a book or with a pen and paper.

Another favorite café, and also a notorious spot visited by many writers and Bohemian types during the Jazz Age, was Café de Flore, the main rival to Les Deux Magots. The café is notable for its classic Art Deco interior, broad menu of French comfort foods, and sunny sidewalk terrace. It has

Far from the restrictions of Prohibition, café customers in Paris could enjoy a glass of wine at La Rotonde.

a proud history for its contribution to the literature of the 1920s and still cultivates its place among the Parisian writing community. In 1994, Café de Flore began handing out an annual literary prize—the Prix de Flore—to promising young authors of French-language literature. Besides a cash prize, the winner gets to drink a glass of the white Pouilly-Fumé wine at the café every day for a year.

Last but certainly not least, La Closerie des Lilas ('Lilac arbor'), also located on the Boulevard du Montparnasse, was once the site of Hemingway's unofficial office in one of the café's red booths.

It also served as a home from home to F. Scott Fitzgerald, Ford Madox Ford, and Gertrude Stein.

These cafés were places where writers, artists, and a variety of hard-working and adventurous people were able to meet, during a time of frenetic creative activity. Paris had become a place for like-minded people to be together, exchange ideas, and make lasting friendships that would lead to inspiration and often lifelong bonds. Not much has changed if you think about it—all around the world, words and art are displayed, shared, and created over a cup of coffee at a café.

Chapter Five
Dinner

Bouillabaisse

The Finest French Chicken

Coq au Vin

Daisy and Tom's Fried Chicken

Nicole Diver's Chicken à la Maryland

Dijon Mustard

Frogs' Legs

"Jugged" Rabbit

T.S. Eliot's Duck à l'Orange

Steak Frites

Boeuf Bourguignon

Petits Farcis

Gnocchi al Virgil Thomson

Bouillabaisse

Fitzgerald gave a recipe for bouillabaisse in *Tender Is the Night*: "The Divers went to Nice and dined on a bouillabaisse, which is a stew of rock fish and small lobsters, highly seasoned with saffron, and a bottle of cold Chablis...."

¾ cup/175 ml olive oil

2 yellow onions, thinly sliced

2 leeks, sliced

3 small tomatoes, peeled, seeded, and chopped

6 garlic cloves, finely chopped

2 sprigs of fennel leaf

1 sprig of fresh thyme

1 sprig of fresh rosemary

1 bay leaf

1 teaspoon orange zest

1 pinch of saffron threads

9 cups/2 liters boiling water

2 lb/1 kg assorted firm white fish fillets (according to seasonal availability and location), cut into chunks

1 lb/450 g mussels, cleaned and debearded

8 very large fresh shrimp/prawns, shell on

salt and freshly ground black pepper

toasted baguette, to serve

rouille, to serve (see right)

SERVES 4

Heat the oil in a large saucepan over low heat. Add the onions, leeks, tomatoes, and garlic and cook, stirring, for a few minutes until the vegetables have softened. Stir in the fennel, herbs, and orange zest.

Add the saffron and boiling water; stir to combine. Season to taste with salt and black pepper. Turn up the heat to high, and boil for about 3 minutes to allow the oil and water to combine.

Reduce the heat to a gentle simmer. Add the chunks of whte fish and cook very gently for a few minutes until only just turning opaque. Add the mussels and prawns and continue to cook gentlry until the mussels open and the prawns are pink and cooked through. The fish will be cooked by this stage.

Taste the bouillabaisse and adjust the seasoning. Discard any mussels that have not opened. Serve the soup immediately in a warmed tureen or individual soup bowls, with toasted slices of baguette with a spoonful of rouille on top.

Quick Rouille

3 anchovy fillets, drained

1 garlic clove

¾ cup/150 g good-quality mayonnaise

finely grated zest and juice of ½ lemon

dash of paprika

pinch of salt and freshly ground black pepper

Pound the anchovies and garlic in a pestle and mortar to make a paste, then mix with the mayonnaise in a bowl. Stir through the lemon zest and juice and paprika and season well to taste.

The Finest French Chicken

The chickens of the Bresse region have long enjoyed a coveted reputation. Much like wine in France, this bird has *appellation d'origine controlee* (AOC) status, reserved for the white chickens of the Bresse breed raised within a legally demarcated region of the historic area and former province of Bresse, in eastern France. Before Hemingway and Fitzgerald left Lyon, where they picked up Scott's car, they had their hotel kitchen pack them a lunch of truffled roast chicken, accompanied by bread and white Macon wine. Seeing as Bresse chickens are hard to come by, and expensive, you may wish to opt for a regular chicken.

Poulet de Bresse

3½-lb/1.5-kg chicken

¾ oz/20 g black truffles, sliced into paper-thin discs

½ tablespoon salt

½ tablespoon freshly ground black pepper

2 tablespoons butter, softened

2 teaspoons Cognac

3 garlic cloves, peeled and halved lengthwise

Serves 4

Prepare the chicken the night before. Loosen the skin of the chicken on the breast and legs, then slide the truffle slices under the skin. Tie the chicken legs together and wrap loosely in plastic wrap/clingfilm. Refrigerate.

Preheat the oven to 400°F (200°C) Gas 6.

Sprinkle the chicken with salt and pepper.

Take a very large piece of foil and rub it with the butter. Pour the cognac into the chicken cavity and add the garlic. Place the chicken on the foil and wrap it up like a present. Place on a baking sheet and bake in the preheated oven for 1 hour, opening up the foil 15 minutes before the end of the cooking time to brown the chicken.

When the chicken is cooked and the juices run clear, transfer the chicken to a serving platter. Serve with buttered egg noodles and a freshly baked baguette (see page 79).

Coq au Vin

The Alice B. Toklas Cookbook, published in 1954, was a major success. She had a deep love of French cooking and a notorious sense of humor. The book is remembered for its recipe for cannabis brownies, but also included Alice's recipe for Coq au Vin, which used white wine rather than red, brandy, and a quantity of pork fat. This recipe is for a more traditional Coq au Vin.

2 young chickens, around 3½ lb/ 1.5 kg each, cut into 4 pieces (2 breasts and 2 legs)

1 yellow onion, sliced

2 carrots, chopped

3 garlic cloves, smashed

20 black peppercorns

bunch of Italian parsley

1 tomato, quartered

2 bottles of inexpensive Bordeaux wine

3 generous tablespoons olive oil

2 tablespoons butter

3 tablespoons all-purpose/plain flour

12 oz/340 g small button mushrooms, trimmed

1 lb/450 g yellow (not white) pearl onions, peeled

pinch of salt

pinch of sugar

SERVES 6–8

In a plastic container large enough to hold both quartered chickens, mix together the chicken pieces, sliced onion, carrots, garlic, peppercorns, parsley, tomato, and wine. Cover and refrigerate for 10–12 hours or overnight.

Preheat the oven to 350°F (175°C) Gas 4.

Remove the chicken from the marinade and pat dry. Strain the vegetables and herbs from the marinade and reserve both separately.

Using a flameproof/ovenproof casserole or pot large enough to hold all the chicken pieces, heat 2 tablespoons of the oil and 1 tablespoon of the butter. Once hot, add the chicken skin side down, allow to brown, then turn over and brown the other side.

Once the chicken is mostly browned, add the reserved marinade vegetables and herbs to the pot and cook for about 5 minutes until the onions are translucent.

Sprinkle the flour over the chicken and vegetables and cook for 1–2 minutes until well mixed in. Add the reserved marinade to the pot and mix well. The sauce should thicken slightly. Cover the pot and transfer to the preheated oven. Cook for 45 minutes or until the chicken is cooked through and the juices run clear.

Remove the chicken from the pot, strain the sauce and discard the vegetables. Return the chicken and sauce to the pot and keep covered until ready to reheat and serve.

Heat the remaining oil in a sauté pan. Add the mushrooms and quickly cook, then add to the chicken.

Place the pearl onions in the sauté pan and add just enough water to cover plus a pinch of salt, a pinch of sugar, and the remaining tablespoon of butter. Cook over medium heat and by

the time the water has evaporated, the onions should be glazed. When they start to brown, remove from the heat and add them to the chicken.

Reheat the chicken before serving. Serve each person a portion of chicken with a spoonful of the sauce with mushrooms and onions. Accompany with boiled potatoes, a lot of French bread, and wine.

Daisy and Tom's Fried Chicken

This recipe dates from 1922, a time when fried chicken was becoming popular in America across every social class. Fried chicken makes a notable appearance in *The Great Gatsby*, which Fitzgerald finished while living in Paris. Perhaps its inclusion was a symptom of homesickness.

"Crossing the porch where we had dined that June night three months before, I came to a small rectangle of light which I guessed was the pantry window. The blind was drawn, but I found a rift at the sill.

Daisy and Tom were sitting opposite each other at the kitchen table, with a plate of cold fried chicken between them and two bottles of ale.

He was talking intently across the table at her, and in his earnestness his hand had fallen upon and covered her own. Once in a while she looked up at him and nodded in agreement."

1 whole fryer chicken, cut into breasts, drumsticks, and thighs, with or without skin

1 tablespoon each salt and freshly ground black pepper, plus more to taste

2 cups/270 g all-purpose/plain flour

leftover bread, processed into breadcrumbs in a food processor (optional)

shortening or oil, for frying

SERVES 4

Sprinkle the chicken pieces evenly with a tablespoon of salt and pepper each. Place the seasoned chicken and flour (and breadcrumbs, if using) in a plastic bag and shake to coat the chicken evenly in flour.

Melt the shortening or heat the oil in a large skillet/frying pan over medium-high heat. Add the chicken to the pan and brown on both sides over medium-high heat, then continue to cook for a further 7–10 minutes until the chicken is cooked through and the juices run clear.

Remove the chicken from the pan, drain on paper towel, and serve warm.

Nicole Diver's Chicken à la Maryland

This dish is inspired by F. Scott Fitzgerald's female antagonist, Nicole Diver in his acclaimed novel, *Tender Is the Night*. Nicole lies on a tranquil beach trying to hold herself together and reassures herself that "everything is all right—if I can finish translating this damn recipe for Chicken à la Maryland into French." I like to believe that after all her work, she was left with this delicious recipe to reward her efforts. This was also rumored to be one of Fitzgerald's favorite dishes and features in Escoffier's 1912 cookbook, *Ma Cuisine*.

4 boneless chicken breasts, cut in half lengthwise

1¾ cups/415 ml buttermilk

6 tablespoons/85 g butter

1 cup/130 g all-purpose/plain flour

2 eggs, beaten

1⅓ cups/100 g dry breadcrumbs

BÉCHAMEL SAUCE

3 tablespoons/40 g butter

3 tablespoons/25 g all-purpose/plain flour

2½ cups/590 ml milk

1 teaspoon salt

⅛ teaspoon freshly grated nutmeg

TO GARNISH

3 tablespoons/40 g butter

2 ripe, firm bananas, peeled and sliced

Dijon mustard (see page 98)

SERVES 4

Place the chicken and the buttermilk in a large, shallow bowl and marinate in the fridge for 1 hour.

Preheat the oven to 375°F (190°C) Gas 5.

Melt the butter in a large roasting pan. Drain the chicken and discard the buttermilk. Dredge each piece of chicken in the flour, then dip in the beaten egg and coat in the breadcrumbs. Arrange the chicken in the roasting pan and bake for 30–40 minutes, turning once, until cooked through and the breadcrumb coating is crispy.

Make the béchamel sauce while the chicken is cooking. In a large saucepan over medium heat, melt the butter and whisk in the flour until it forms a smooth paste. Continue whisking and cook for about 2 minutes, then gradually add the milk, a little at a time. Continue whisking and cook until the sauce is completely heated through, smooth, and thickened. Remove from the heat and season with salt and nutmeg.

To make the banana garnish, melt the butter in a large skillet/frying pan over medium heat. Sauté the banana slices until golden brown on all sides.

To serve, arrange the chicken on warm plates, drizzling the béchamel sauce over, and then garnish the plate with a few slices of sautéed banana. Serve with the Dijon mustard on the side.

Dijon Mustard

1 cup/235 ml dry Champagne or dry white wine

½ large onion, chopped

2 garlic cloves, finely chopped

½ cup/55 g mustard powder

1½ tablespoons honey

1½ teaspoons vegetable or canola oil

1 teaspoon salt

MAKES 1 CUP/235 ML

Note: the mustard needs at least 8 hours to set. Try to make it the night before using, but it is even better if left to mature in the refrigerator for a few weeks.

In a small, non-stick saucepan over medium-high heat, combine the Champagne, onion and garlic. Slowly heat to boiling, then lower the heat and simmer for 5 minutes.

Remove from the heat and let cool for a few minutes. Strain the mixture into a clean pan, discarding the onion and garlic.

Add the mustard powder to the liquid, stirring constantly until smooth. Blend in the honey, oil, and salt. Heat slowly until thickened (be aware that this is a strong smelling mixture), stirring constantly.

Pour into a sterilized glass jar and let cool (ideally leave it on the work surface at room temperature overnight). Refrigerate for 2–8 weeks to age the flavor before using.

Frogs' Legs

Zelda Fitzgerald was also a writer herself and *The Collected Writings of Zelda Fitzgerald* was published posthumously. Her stories are very autobiographical, such as the novel *Save Me the Waltz*, which she wrote in six weeks while residing in a psychiatric facility in Baltimore in 1932. The story is about a Southern girl named Alabama (echoing Zelda's home state), who decides to become a ballet dancer. The classic French dish of frogs' legs makes an appearance in this story. And why not? The cuisine of Escoffier was being replicated further and further afield, and French food was becoming the world's best-loved cuisine.

2½ cups/115 g panko
or breadcrumbs

1 cup/130 g all-purpose/plain flour

½ cup/75 g cornmeal/polenta

½ small onion, finely chopped

2 teaspoons salt

1 tablespoon freshly ground
black pepper

2 eggs

½ cup/120 ml milk

canola or vegetable oil, for frying

24 frogs' legs, skin removed

SERVES 4

In a large bag, combine the panko/breadcrumbs, flour, cornmeal, onions, salt, and pepper. Shake well together.

In a separate bowl, mix together the eggs and milk.

Heat about a ½-in/1-cm depth of oil in a large skillet/frying pan over medium-high heat.

Dredge the frogs' legs, one by one, through the egg mixture and then through the flour mixture until well coated. Carefully place them in the oil and cook for about 4 minutes each side until golden brown. Reduce the heat if the legs begin to brown too rapidly.

When the legs are an even golden color, remove from the heat and drain or blot off the excess oil using paper towel. Serve immediately.

"Jugged" Rabbit

Jugged hare was a family favorite of Alice B. Toklas and a dinner she made often for her partner, Gertrude Stein, and literary figures such as the Fitzgeralds, who frequented their famous dinner parties.
It was a dish that required a lot of preparation, starting a day or two before it was to be served, and traditional versions included the hare's blood and liver. This much simpler alternative, made with rabbit, is more likely to appeal to contemporary palates, and those with busy schedules.

1 lb/450 g bacon, diced

2½ lb/1.1 kg rabbit meat, deboned and cut into stew-sized pieces

½ teaspoon salt

¼ cup/35 g all-purpose/plain flour, plus 2 tablespoons for thickening

2 carrots, chopped

2 garlic cloves, finely chopped

½ cup/60 g finely chopped shallots

1 cup/235 ml dry red wine

1 cup/235 ml chicken broth/stock

1 tablespoon redcurrant jelly

12 black peppercorns, crushed

2 bay leaves

¼ teaspoon dried rosemary, crushed

2 teaspoons freshly squeezed lemon juice

2 or 3 sprigs of fresh thyme

SERVES 4

Fry the bacon in a large, deep skillet/frying pan over medium heat until cooked. Remove the bacon from the pan and drain on paper towel. Set aside to cool.

Sprinkle the rabbit with the salt, then coat well with the flour. Discard the excess flour. Brown the rabbit in the bacon fat remaining in the pan. Remove the rabbit from the pan when it becomes golden in color and set aside. Leave 2 tablespoons of the fat in the pan.

Add the carrots to the pan and sauté for 2 minutes, then add the garlic and shallots and sauté for 3–4 minutes or until the carrots are tender. Stir in the wine and chicken broth/stock. Bring the mixture to a boil, then stir in the redcurrant jelly, peppercorns, bay leaves, and rosemary.

Return the rabbit and bacon to the pan. Heat the stew until boiling, then reduce the heat to low. Cover the pan and cook for about 1½ hours or until the rabbit is tender and moist.

Remove and discard the bay leaves. Remove the rabbit from the stew and cover to keep warm.

Stir the lemon juice into the pan. Combine 3 tablespoons of water with the extra 2 tablespoons of flour and mix together until they are combined. Stir the water-flour mixture into the stew to thicken, keeping the heat at low. Stir in the sprigs of thyme and mix the rabbit back into the stew. Serve hot.

T.S. Eliot's Duck à l'Orange

It's said that something everyone should accomplish in life is at least one dish that is their staple. For poet T. S. Eliot, it was his Duck à l'Orange. Scott and Eliot were fans of each other's work. When *The Great Gatsby* was released in 1925, critics called it a dud, but Eliot wrote to Scott to compliment him. Fitzgerald was delighted and wrote back to Eliot: "I can't express just how good your letter made me feel... it was easily the nicest thing that's happened to me in connection with *Gatsby*."

I like to think the two men would have enjoyed at least one Duck à l'Orange together.

2 duck breasts, halved

1 cup/235 ml duck broth (see page 104)

2 tablespoons orange liqueur

1 tablespoon sherry vinegar

1 tablespoon Seville orange marmalade, or more to taste (see page 105)

2 teaspoons grated orange zest

pinch of cayenne pepper

orange slices, to garnish

1 teaspoon all-purpose/plain flour

1 tablespoon butter

salt

SERVES 2

Score the duck almost all the way through the skin and fat on the diagonal in a crosshatch pattern. Generously season with salt, rubbing it into each breast. Let the duck rest, skin-side up, at room temperature, for 15 minutes.

Whisk the duck broth, orange liqueur, sherry vinegar, marmalade, orange zest, and cayenne pepper together in a small bowl.

Pat the duck dry with paper towel; re-season the skin side with salt.

Heat a heavy skillet/frying pan over medium heat. Place the duck breasts in the pan, skin side down, and cook for 5–6 minutes. Flip the duck breasts over and cook on the other side until they start to firm and are reddish-pink and juicy in the center, about 4 minutes. An instant-read thermometer inserted into the center should read 140°F (60°C). Transfer the duck to a plate to rest. Cook the orange slices in the same pan for a minute or two, then remove and set to one side. Pour any rendered duck fat into a glass jar, leaving just a thin coating on the bottom of the pan.

Return the pan to medium heat and whisk the flour into the pan; cook and stir for about 1 minute until the flour is completely incorporated into the fat remaining in the pan. Pour the orange mixture into the pan and bring to a boil. Cook for 3–5 minutes until the sauce thickens and is reduced. Reduce the heat to low. When the orange mixture stops bubbling, add the butter and stir until the butter is completely melted and incorporated into the sauce, about 1 minute. Season with salt to taste.

Slice the duck breasts across the grain, arrange on a plate, garnish with the orange slices and spoon the orange sauce over.

Duck Broth

Preheat the oven to 400°F (200°C) Gas 6.

Place the duck carcass in a large roasting pan and drizzle with olive oil; roast for about 1 hour until well browned.

When the bones are browned, transfer them to a large stockpot and cover with cold water, leaving 2–3 in/5–7.5 cm of room at the top of the pot. If the roasting pan has a lot of fat in it, drain it off. Add some more water to the roasting pan, scrape up any browned bits with a wooden spoon, and add to the stockpot.

Cover the pot and bring it to a boil, but as soon as it hits a boil, drop the heat to a bare simmer and move the pot lid slightly ajar. Let this cook very, very gently (more steaming than simmering) for as long as you can—I leave it overnight.

When you are ready to add the vegetables, toss them all in and stir to combine. Note that this is the only time you stir this stock. Let them simmer gently for 2 hours.

Turn off the heat and strain the stock—I use a big container (such as a large plastic tub) and over this I set a strainer, lined with paper towel. Using a ladle, ladle the stock into the strainer so it strains through the paper towel. Doing it this way keeps the stock very clear.

Your broth is ready now. Season with salt to taste, adding a little at a time. You can further concentrate flavors by simmering the strained stock for as long as you like. Check the flavor every 15 minutes or so.

Pour into Mason preserving jars and refrigerate for up to 2 weeks, or freeze for up to 9 months. If you freeze, leave at least 1½ in/4 cm of headspace in the jars or they will crack. You can also pressure-can your stock at 10 psi for 25 minutes (follow your canner's directions for this).

1 duck carcass

olive oil, for drizzling

1 generous tablespoon each of salt and freshly ground black pepper

1 onion, chopped

2 celery stalks, chopped

2 carrots, chopped

1 fennel bulb, chopped (optional)

1 large sprig of fresh rosemary

2 teaspoons dried thyme

3 bay leaves

1 tablespoon black peppercorns, cracked

1 tablespoon juniper berries

Seville Orange Marmalade

3 lb/1.3 kg Seville oranges

4½ lb/2 kg granulated sugar

MAKES ABOUT 4 LARGE OR 8 SMALL JARS

Wash the oranges. Using a sharp knife, score the peel of each orange into quarters and remove without damaging the fruit. Slice the peel thinly or thickly, depending on your taste, and put into a very large cast-iron pot. Squeeze the peeled oranges into the pot, taking care to reserve any pips. Deseed the remaining flesh. Chop the flesh and add it to the peel. Put the pips into a mesh tea ball or a muslin bag and add to the pot. Fill the pot with 3 quarts/2.5 liters of cold water. Cover the pot and let it sit for 24 hours.

Bring the contents of the pot to a boil, then remove the lid and let it simmer for 45 minutes or until the peel is soft and the colors are translucent.

Remove the bag or ball of pips from the pot, squeezing or scraping it for every last bit of pectin. Add the sugar to the fruit mixture and stir well. Raise the heat and bring the marmalade to a boil. Let cook for anywhere from 15–60 minutes, stirring occasionally, until the marmalade forms a thin skin when spooned onto a little plate that has been chilled in the freezer. Ladle the marmalade into sterilized jars, close them tightly, and turn them upside-down to cool overnight.

Steak Frites

The comfort food of wealthy Parisians, Steak Frites is a meal enjoyed at any time of day and was another favorite of T. S. Eliot's. This recipe is for a quick and simple Steak Frites that you will still find around Paris at many of the usual haunts, such as Les Deux Magots.

1¼ lb/500 g floury potatoes

sunflower oil, for frying

salt

1 lb/450 g beef sirloin grilling steak, cut into 4 portions

2 teaspoons freshly chopped thyme

freshly ground black pepper

DIPPING SAUCE

⅓ cup/75 ml mayonnaise

1 tablespoon freshly chopped chives

2 teaspoons Dijon mustard

1 teaspoon freshly squeezed lemon juice

SERVES 4

Peel the potatoes and cut into ¼ in/5mm slices, then into batons ¼ in/5mm wide. Put into a bowl of iced water for at least 5 minutes.

Fill a large saucepan one-third full with the sunflower oil. Heat the oil to 375°F (190°C) or until a cube of bread browns in the oil in 30 seconds. (If preferred, you can use a deep-fat fryer, following the manufacturer's instructions.)

Drain the potato batons and pat dry with paper towel. Working in batches, and using tongs or the deep-fryer basket, carefully lower 2 large handfuls of potato batons into the oil and fry for about 4 minutes. Remove with tongs or a slotted spoon, or lift out the basket, and drain on paper towel. Repeat until all the batons have been cooked. Skim any debris off the top of the oil, reheat to the same temperature, and fry the batons a second time until crisp and golden, about 2 minutes. Remove and drain on paper towel again, then sprinkle with salt. Keep the frites hot in the oven until ready to serve.

Meanwhile, sprinkle the steak with thyme, salt, and pepper. Heat the remaining oil in a large skillet/frying pan over medium-high heat. Cook the steak, turning once, until medium-rare, about 6 minutes. Transfer to a cutting board and tent with foil; let stand for 10 minutes.

In small bowl, combine the mayonnaise, chives, mustard, and lemon juice. Serve with the steak and frites as a dipping sauce for the potatoes.

Boeuf Bourguignon

Boeuf Bourguignon, a beef stew with roots in the Burgundy region of France, is a homely, hearty, and comfortable dish. It's a classic, a favorite of Fitzgerald's—who would enjoy it at Paris's famous Polidor restaurant—and also a favorite of many writers who frequented the literary salon of Stein and Toklas in Paris.

1 bottle of Burgundy wine

2 tablespoons brandy

4 onions, 2 thinly sliced and 2 chopped

2 carrots, chopped

2 sprigs of parsley

1 bay leaf

3 garlic cloves, crushed

10 whole black peppercorns

1 teaspoon salt

2 lb/900 g chuck roast /braising steak cut into large cubes

4 tablespoons olive oil

4 oz/115 g bacon, cubed

3 tablespoons all-purpose/plain flour

1 tablespoon tomato paste

1¼ cups/300 ml veal stock

4 tablespoons/60 g butter

1 lb/450 g mushrooms, sliced

salt and freshly ground black pepper

SERVES 4–6

In a large bowl, combine the wine, brandy, sliced onions, carrots, parsley, bay leaf, 1 crushed garlic clove, peppercorns, and salt. Mix well and add the cubed beef. Cover and marinate in the fridge for 2 days.

Preheat the oven to 300°F (150°C) Gas 2.

Strain the meat from the vegetables/marinade. Set aside.

Dry the meat with paper towel. Heat 2 tablespoons of the oil in a large skillet/frying pan over medium-high heat. Add a few pieces of the meat and sauté for 10 minutes, or until browned on all sides. Using a slotted spoon, transfer the meat to a medium bowl and set aside. Repeat for the remaining pieces, in small batches each time.

When all the meat is browned, using the same pan, add the bacon and sauté until lightly browned. Transfer the bacon to the bowl with the meat. Drain the pan and return it to the heat.

Pour 1 cup/235 ml of the reserved marinade (without vegetables) into the pan to deglaze, scraping the bottom to loosen up all the little bits. Return this liquid to the reserved marinade.

Heat the remaining oil in the pan. Add the onion and carrot from the marinade, along with the additional chopped onion, and sauté for 5 minutes, or until tender. Transfer this mixture to the bowl with the meat and bacon, using a slotted spoon, and return the pan to the heat. Add the flour to the pan, combining it with the oil and stirring until well mixed and brown, about 2 minutes.

Add the tomato paste, remaining crushed garlic, veal stock, reserved marinade, and salt and pepper to taste. Bring to a boil and whisk to remove any flour lumps. Add this to the meat and vegetable mixture. Place the entire mixture in a 9 x 13-in/23 x 33-cm baking dish.

Bake in the preheated oven for 3 hours, stirring occasionally and adding water as needed. Season with salt and pepper to taste.

About 15 minutes before the meat is ready, melt the butter in the skillet/frying pan over medium-high heat. Add the mushrooms and sauté for 5–10 minutes, or until lightly browned. Stir them into the stew and serve.

Petits Farcis

You will find variations of this French staple in restaurants throughout the Côte d'Azur. The classic version uses pork sausage or a combination of pork and beef, but this dish can easily be made vegetarian by replacing the meat with cooked rice. If possible, try to find "cocktail" tomatoes as they call them in France, which are a bit larger than cherry tomatoes. If they're not available, the best bet is to go for regular tomatoes. Use Herbes de Provence if you can find them. This is a mixture of rosemary, thyme, and a variety of other herbs such as marjoram, savory, or basil. It's also fine to just use a little fresh or dried thyme.

1 lb/450 g ground beef or pork

breadcrumbs made from 1 thick slice of white bread

1 tablespoon freshly chopped parsley

3 garlic cloves, finely chopped

1 shallot, finely chopped

2 teaspoons dried herbes de Provence or thyme

½ teaspoon salt

freshly ground black pepper

2 eggs

2 medium zucchini/courgettes, cut lengthwise and hollowed out

2 small eggplant/aubergines, cut lengthwise and hollowed out

10 tomatoes, cut in half, insides and seeds scooped out

2 tablespoons olive oil

SERVES 4

Preheat the oven to 190°C (375°F) Gas 5.

Combine the ground meat with the breadcrumbs, parsley, garlic, shallot, dried herbs, salt, and pepper. Using your hands, mix the ingredients together. Crack in the eggs and mix again until the ingredients are thoroughly blended.

Using a spoon, stuff the hollowed-out zucchini/courgettes, eggplant/aubergines, and tomatoes with the meat mixture.

Coat the bottom of two baking pans each with about a teaspoon of the olive oil. Arrange the stuffed zucchini/courgettes and eggplant/aubergines in one pan, and the stuffed tomatoes in the other. Drizzle with the remaining olive oil.

Bake the zucchini/courgettes and eggplant/aubergines for about 1 hour and the tomatoes for about 45 minutes, or until the meat is browned and the vegetables are tender. It's tricky to get this balance right—you want the vegetables to be tender without overcooking the meat, so check occasionally while they are cooking.

Delicious served with rice and a glass of rosé wine.

Gnocchi al Virgil Thomson

Virgil Thomson was an American composer who made his way to Paris during the 1920s. He would often premiere his work to Gertrude Stein and Alice B. Toklas, along with a cast of characters that included George Gershwin, Cole Porter, T. S. Eliot and of course, Scott and Zelda Fitzgerald. This dish was a favorite of his and he eventually passed his recipe for it on to Alice B. Toklas, who included it in her cookbook. This is the classic version of the recipe.

1 lb/450 g yellow potatoes

1 cup/150 g all-purpose/plain flour

1 egg, beaten

5 tablespoons/70 g butter

1 clove garlic, crushed and finely chopped (optional)

6 tablespoons grated Parmesan cheese

salt and freshly ground black pepper

pinch of nutmeg

SERVES 4

Preheat the oven to 375°F (190°C) Gas 5.

Bake the potatoes in the preheated oven until you can squeeze them with your hands—they should be soft. Set aside briefly to cool to a temperature at which they can be handled. Cut each potato in half, scoop out the insides into a bowl and mash.

Scatter most of the flour onto a clean work surface, make a well in the center and drop the mashed potatoes into the well. Add the beaten egg and gently combine all of the ingredients to form a dough.

Cut the mixture in half and roll into two long ropes of dough, then cut these into 1-in/2.5-cm pieces to create small dumplings. Place these on a baking sheet or cutting board sprinkled with flour and if so desired, indent the tops using a fork. If you wish, the gnocchi can be frozen on a baking sheet at this stage.

Bring a pan of salted water to the boil. Drop the gnocchi in and remove them with a slotted spoon when they start to float to the surface—this will only take about 1 minute.

While the gnocchi cook, melt the butter in a pan with the garlic, if using. Place the cooked gnocchi in individual serving dishes. Toss with melted butter (after removing the garlic) and sprinkle over the grated Parmesan. Season with salt and pepper to taste, and finish with a pinch of nutmeg.

Chefs de Paris

In 1920, the famed chef Auguste Escoffier retired. For years he had shaped, molded, and structured French cuisine, and made France the epicenter for teaching the world how to cook. On his retirement, the baton passed to a new generation.

While the great master chefs of the 1920s most certainly had Escoffier to thank for their heritage, many of them would have learned their practical skills from Henri-Paul Pellaprat, the man in charge of the famed Le Cordon Bleu cookery school in Paris. By 1927, Le Cordon Bleu had evolved from being an exclusively French institution. Students from all over the world were in attendance, taking classes led by teachers and chefs who were also not all French.

Born in 1869, Pellaprat began cooking at the age of 12. With hard work and natural talent he flourished quickly and went on to direct some of the finest kitchens in France. He later took a position as a professor at Le Cordon Bleu and taught at the school for 40 years, during which time he wrote his master work *L'Art Culinaire Moderne*. Pellaprat's cookbook was translated into five languages, and when it appeared in English (as *The Great Book of French Cookery*), it was hailed as "the most comprehensive, authoritative, and up-to-date book on French cooking and gastronomy ever written." In 1935 Pellaprat

retired, but Le Cordon Bleu continued to expand and develop.

Le Cordon Bleu was an institution that, in many ways, taught the world to cook. The school published one of the first cooking magazines. Budding chefs and home cooks alike would buy the magazine, hoping to learn to cook like the professionals. Even Julia Child got her start at Le Cordon Bleu, although not for many years after the Jazz Age ended.

American chefs, as well as bartenders (see page 144), arrived in Paris fresh from New York, bringing the food of America with them. They would go on to create fusion food, encompassing the best of both worlds: classic French cuisine married with the rebellious taste of America. France had just started falling into step, using Escoffier's kitchen tactics, when a young American by the name of James Beard arrived in France.

Born in Portland, Oregon, Beard lived abroad for several years, studying singing and theater. As a friend of Gertrude Stein and her partner Alice B. Toklas, he mixed in the same circles as Fitzgerald during his time in France.

Beard returned to the USA in 1927, and in 1935 his life took a different turn when he and his friend Bill Rhodes opened a small grocery

Auguste Escoffier, on the left, outside a Paris café.

store called Hors d'Oeuvre, Inc. In 1937 his first cookbook, *Hors d'Oeuvre and Canapés*, was published. He went on to appear in the first cookery program on US television, and to publish many other cookbooks, and today the James Beard Foundation presents awards for culinary excellence in his name.

Chapter Six
Desserts and Baking

Butter Cookies

Alice B. Toklas (together with her partner Getrude Stein) was one of the most famous hostesses of the Jazz Age, bringing together artists, writers, and other cultural luminaries. Not only did she throw a great party, she also made a mean butter cookie.

2½ cups/340 g all-purpose/plain flour

½ cup plus 1 tablespoon/115 g superfine/caster sugar, plus extra for sprinkling

1 vanilla bean, split lengthwise and seeds scraped out

1 cup/225 g butter, cut into 1-in/ 2.5-cm cubes

MAKES 20–24

Preheat the oven to 325°F (160°C) Gas 3.

Mix the flour, sugar, and vanilla seeds together in a large bowl, then rub in the butter as if you were making pastry. Use the tips of your fingers and ensure that all the butter has been rubbed in— it should resemble sand and be a little finer than if making pastry. This can also be done in a food processor by pulsing flour, sugar, and butter until the desired sand-like consistency is achieved.

Turn the dough out onto a lightly floured surface and knead. The heat from your hands will make the butter melt and come together to a smooth consistency.

Divide the shortbread dough into two equal parts and shape into balls, then flatten them out into two rounds, about 7 in/18 cm in diameter and ¼ in/5 mm thick, using the heel of your hand.

Mark the top of each round into equal triangular portions, then prick the tops all over with a fork, making patterns if you wish. Crimp the edges as you would a pie crust to make a decorative edge, then transfer to a well-greased baking tray or cookie sheet. Sprinkle the tops with sugar.

Bake in the preheated oven for 20–30 minutes until a light golden color. You want to keep the color of these cookies on the light side and make sure you don't brown them or they will be dry. Remove from the oven, set aside and let cool before cutting into triangles as marked.

Enjoy with tea or coffee with your literary buddies as you talk philosophy and politics.

Peach Melba

This iconic dessert has been around since the late nineteenth century, when it was invented by the French chef Auguste Escoffier, a legendary figure of French cuisine, at the Savoy Hotel in London. He created this dish in honor of the Australian soprano Nellie Melba. Despite its origins, it is a French dessert that is, was, and always will be a staple. With Zelda Fitzgerald's penchant for peaches, it's a safe bet that she enjoyed a few of these in Paris.

3 cups/600 g sugar

pinch of salt

1½ tablespoons lemon juice

1 vanilla bean, split lengthwise (don't scrape out the seeds)

4 large peaches

ice cream, to serve (see page 122)

mint leaves, to decorate (optional)

RASPBERRY SAUCE

2 cups/300 g raspberries

3 tablespoons confectioner's/ icing sugar

½ tablespoon freshly squeezed lemon juice

SERVES 4

Put the sugar, salt, lemon juice, and vanilla bean in a medium, wide saucepan with 3 cups water and set over low heat. Heat until the sugar dissolves, then increase the temperature to medium-high and bring to a boil. Let the mixture boil for 3–4 minutes, then turn the heat down to a simmer.

Cut the peaches in half. Add the peaches to the sugar syrup and poach for about 2 minutes on each side—depending on how ripe the peaches are, they may need an extra 30–60 seconds. Test with the point of a sharp knife to see if they are soft. When soft, use a slotted spoon to remove them from the pan and place on a plate. You may need to poach the peaches in batches.

When the peaches are poached but still warm, peel off the skins (they should come off easily) and remove the stones. Set aside.

In a blender or food processor, combine the raspberries, confectioner's/icing sugar, and lemon juice. Add 1 tablespoon of water if you want a thinner sauce. Process until the mixture is combined and smooth. Push through a strainer to remove the raspberry seeds.

Remove the ice cream from the freezer about 10 minutes before serving, to allow it to soften.

To assemble, sit two peach halves on a small plate alongside a quenelle or scoop of French vanilla ice cream. Spoon the raspberry sauce on top. Garnish with mint leaves if you wish.

French Ice Cream

Established in 1761, À la Mère de Famille is Paris's oldest sweet shop, known for its fine ice cream, cakes, sweets, and chocolates. This recipe for French ice cream uses a cream and egg base. You can modify it to make lemon or strawberry ice cream, and it also doesn't hurt to just throw a few chocolate chips in there after churning....

VANILLA BASE

2 cups/475 ml whole milk

2½ cups/590 ml heavy/
double cream

2 vanilla beans, halved lengthwise

8 large egg yolks

¾ cup/150 g sugar

pinch of salt

3 tablespoons Kirsch liqueur (optional)

LEMON FLAVOR

1 cup/235 ml freshly squeezed
lemon juice

STRAWBERRY FLAVOR

1–2 cups/140–280 g strawberries,
chopped

2 tablespoons sugar

MAKES 1 QUART/950 ML

Over medium-high heat, mix the milk, cream, and vanilla beans in a pan. Let the mixture become hot, but do not let it simmer or scald. Remove from the heat, cover with a lid and let stand for 25 minutes. After it has steeped, remove the vanilla beans.

Put the egg yolks, sugar, and salt into the bowl of an electric mixer. Using a whisk attachment, beat on high speed for 3–4 minutes until the yolk mixture has tripled in consistency, is a pale yellow, and the whisk leaves a "ribbon" trail when lifted out.

With the mixer on medium speed, slowly pour 1 cup/235 ml of the milk mixture into the yolk mixture. Beat to combine. Repeat until all the milk mixture is incorporated.

Transfer the mixture to saucepan. Cook over medium-high heat, stirring constantly, until it is thick enough to coat the back of a wooden spoon and an instant-read thermometer registers 350°F (180°C), about 5–7 minutes. You don't want the heat to be so hot that it cooks the eggs at the bottom of the pan, so make sure you are stirring consistently.

Pour the custard through a medium-mesh sieve into a bowl set in an ice-water bath. Let cool completely, stirring often. When cool, add the Kirsch (although German, it's used in various ice creams in France). Transfer to an ice-cream maker and freeze according to the manufacturer's directions.

For lemon ice cream: add the lemon juice to the custard base after it cools.

For strawberry ice cream: before making the custard base, combine the strawberries with the sugar. Macerate together and set aside for at least 1 hour. After the ice cream base has cooled, stir in the strawberries and freeze the ice cream.

Daisy's Lemon Cakes

When Gatsby engineers a meeting with Daisy by asking Nick to invite her to tea, his desire to impress is obvious. Unfortunately one detail is not covered—Nick is only able to provide shop-bought lemon cakes.

"I took him into the pantry, where he looked a little reproachfully at the Finn. Together we scrutinized the twelve lemon cakes from the delicatessen shop. 'Will they do?' I asked. 'Of course, of course! They're fine!' and he added hollowly, '...old sport.'"
The Great Gatsby

2 cups/260 g all-purpose/plain flour, plus extra for dusting

2½ teaspoons baking powder

¼ teaspoon salt

⅔ cup/150 g unsalted butter, at room temperature, plus extra for greasing

1 cup/200 g granulated sugar

½ teaspoon vanilla extract

3 large eggs

⅔ cup/150 ml whole milk

1½ tablespoons finely grated lemon zest

mint leaves, to decorate

GLAZE
⅔ cup/90 g confectioner's/icing sugar

⅓ cup/90 ml freshly squeezed lemon juice

pink and/or yellow food coloring (optional)

MAKES 20

Preheat the oven to 350°F (175°C) Gas 4. Grease and lightly flour 20 muffin cups with a diameter of 2½-in/6.5-cm.

Combine the flour, baking powder, and salt in a bowl and set aside.

Beat the butter in the bowl of an electric mixer until smooth. Add the sugar and beat until combined. Add the vanilla extract and the eggs, one at a time, beating well after each addition. Alternately add the flour mixture in three parts and the milk in two, beating on low–medium speed after each addition just until combined. Stir in the lemon zest. Spoon the batter into the prepared muffin cups.

Transfer to the preheated oven and bake for 20–25 minutes, or until a wooden toothpick inserted in the centers comes out clean. Cool in the pans on wire racks for 5 minutes. Remove the cakes from the pans and place on wire racks set over waxed paper.

To make the glaze, stir together the sugar and lemon juice (and food coloring, if using) in a small mixing bowl. Brush the mixture over the warm cakes until all is absorbed. Cool completely. Cover and store in the fridge for up to 5 days or in an airtight container in the freezer for up to 2 months.

To serve, decorate with mint leaves.

Riviera Fruit Salad

This mix of seasonal summer fruits is the perfect refreshment and accompaniment to a late brunch or beach picnic, or in a glass with ice and Champagne.

1 ripe cantaloupe melon, preferably a Charentais

½ cup/75 g each of seasonal summer fruit such as raspberries, blueberries, cherries, and strawberries

¼ cup/40 g each of red and green grapes

freshly squeezed juice of 2 limes

freshly chopped mint

sugar (optional)

SERVES 4

Cut the melon in half and scoop out the seeds. Using a melon baller, scoop out flesh into balls and place in a mixing bowl.

Add the berries, grapes, lime juice, and chopped mint to the mixing bowl. Mix gently. Add sugar if needed. Leave for 10 minutes for the flavors to mingle.

Fill up four dessert bowls or sundae glasses with the fruit salad, and place them on dessert plates to serve.

Buttered Tea Cakes

The Great Gatsby was published when F. Scott Fitzgerald was 28 years old. Full of gusto, he sent a copy to one of his favorite authors, 63-year-old Edith Wharton. In return, she invited him and Zelda to tea at her home outside Paris.

Zelda refused to go, so Fitzgerald invited Teddy Chandler, a mutual friend who would later become a music composer. Fitzgerald got drunk on the way and upon arrival, he found the tea party boring by his standards, and behaved badly. Wharton recorded her impressions of the afternoon in her diary: "To tea, Teddy Chandler and Scott Fitzgerald, the novelist—awful."

This recipe is for French tea cakes, or madeleines, the kind of thing likely to have been served at Wharton's "boring" tea party.

½ cup/115 g butter, softened

4 eggs

1½ teaspoons vanilla extract

¼ teaspoon *fleur de sel* or coarse sea salt

⅔ cup/130 g sugar, plus extra for sprinkling

1 cup/130 g all-purpose/plain flour

2 tablespoons lemon zest

¼ cup/60 g butter, softened (to spread on the cakes)

MAKES 12

Preheat the oven to 375°F (190°C) Gas 5. Butter and flour a 12-hole madeleine tray.

Melt the butter and let it cool to room temperature.

In an electric mixer, beat the eggs, vanilla, and salt at high speed until light. Beating constantly, gradually add the sugar and continue beating at high speed for 5–10 minutes until the mixture is thick and pale and a ribbon "trail" is left when the beaters are lifted.

Sift the flour into the egg mixture one third at a time, gently folding it in after each addition. Add the lemon zest and pour the melted butter around the edge of the batter. Quickly but gently fold the butter into the batter. Spoon the batter into the prepared molds.

Bake in the preheated oven for 14–17 minutes, or until the cakes are golden and the tops spring back when gently pressed with your fingertip.

Use the tip of a knife to loosen the madeleines from the pan and invert onto a wire cooling rack. Immediately sprinkle the warm cakes with sugar. Spread with butter to serve.

Madeleines are best eaten on the day they are baked, but leftover madeleines are wonderful dunked into coffee or tea.

Pistachio and Strawberry Macarons

French macarons are a dainty treat that was first introduced to France in 1533, by Italian pastry chefs brought to the country by Catherine de Medici when she came to marry Henry II of France. In Paris, the go-to place to get a macaron is luxury baker and confectioner Ladurée, established in 1862.

½ cup/50 g finely ground almonds

½ cup/50 g finely ground pistachios*

1½ cups/200 g confectioners'/
icing sugar

3 egg whites, at room temperature

¼ teaspoon salt

3 tablespoons/40g superfine/
caster sugar

green food coloring paste

STRAWBERRY-VANILLA BUTTERCREAM

½ cup/115 g unsalted butter,
at room temperature

1¾–2 cups/230–260 g
confectioners'/icing sugar, sifted

3 tablespoons strawberry jam

½ tablespoon vanilla extract

2 tablespoons milk or cream

⅛ teaspoon salt

*Pistachios can be ground in a
coffee grinder or food processor until
they have the consistency of flour.
Or use pistachio flour, available from
some delicatessens and specialist
food stores.

MAKES 20

Line a baking sheet with parchment paper.

Tip the ground almonds and pistachios and the confectioners'/icing sugar into the bowl of a food processor and blend them for about 30 seconds, until combined thoroughly. Sift to remove any large lumps. Set aside.

Add the salt to the egg whites. Beat with an electric hand-held mixer or whisk on medium until the whites are foamy and will only just hold a stiff peak. Continue to beat on medium speed while adding the superfine/caster sugar in teaspoonfuls, making sure the sugar is completely incorporated before adding the next spoonful. After adding all the superfine/caster sugar, add a small amount of green food coloring paste, by dipping a cocktail stick in the paste and then drawing it through the egg white mixture. Beat on medium-high until the meringue is thick and glossy and the color is distributed evenly.

Scrape down the sides of the mixing bowl. With a large metal spoon, fold in the almonds/pistachios/sugar mixture until well combined and smooth. The mixture should drop from the spoon in a smooth mass when it is ready.

Preheat the oven to 325°F (170°C) Gas 3.

Using a prepared pastry bag, pipe 40 round macaron shells, 2 in/5 cm in diameter, onto the lined baking sheet, about ½ in/1 cm apart. Leave the macarons for at least 15 minutes, and up to 1 hour, so that they form a dry shell on the outside. Test for this by touching them gently with a fingertip: they should not be sticky or wet.

Bake the macarons one sheet at a time on the middle shelf of the oven for 10 minutes, until the tops are firm and the bottoms dry. Remove from the oven and allow to cool on the baking sheet before

gently peeling from the parchment paper. Make sure the macarons are completely cool before filling.

To make the buttercream, in a mixer fitted with a paddle, combine the butter with the confectioners'/ icing sugar, ½ cup at a time, until well mixed and fluffy. Add the strawberry jam and vanilla extract and beat on high for 20–30 seconds. Add the milk or cream, a little at a time, until the buttercream has reached the desired consistency, stiff enough to spread or pipe on to the macarons without spreading. Add the salt and combine well. Spoon or pipe into the middle of the flat underside of half the macarons. Gently top the buttercream with the remaining macarons.

Pineapple Sherbet with Figs

The Divers' famous dinner party scene in *Tender Is the Night* was inspired by evenings at Gerald and Sara Murphy's Villa America in Cap d'Antibes. On one such occasion, Fitzgerald seemed to be under some compulsion to spoil the evening—perhaps on account of his hatred of being ignored. He started inauspiciously by walking up to one of the guests, a young writer, and asking him in a loud, jocular tone whether he was a homosexual. The man quietly replied "Yes," and Fitzgerald retreated in temporary embarrassment. When dessert came, Fitzgerald picked a sherbet-coated fig from a bowl of pineapple sherbet and threw it at the Princesse de Caraman-Chimay, a house guest of the Murphys' friend and neighbor, the Princesse de Poix. It hit her between the shoulder blades; she stiffened for a moment and then went on talking as though nothing had happened. Then Fitzgerald, apparently still feeling that not enough attention was being paid to him, began throwing Sara's gold-flecked Venetian wine glasses over the garden wall. He had smashed three of them this way before Gerald stopped him. As the party was breaking up, Gerald went up to Scott and told him that he would not be welcome in their house for three weeks—a term of banishment that was observed to the day.

½ cup/100 g sugar

1 pineapple, cored, trimmed, puréed in a blender, and forced through a fine sieve (about 3 cups/170 g strained purée)

1½ cups/350 ml milk, well chilled

2 tablespoons freshly squeezed lemon juice

pinch of salt

4 figs, chopped, to serve

MAKES 1 QUART/950 ML

In a small saucepan combine the sugar with ½ cup/120 ml water. Bring the mixture to a boil, then simmer for 5 minutes. Let the sugar syrup cool completely.

In a bowl whisk together the pineapple purée, the cooled sugar syrup, milk, lemon juice, and salt. Chill the mixture until it is cold, then freeze in an ice-cream machine according to the manufacturer's instructions.

Serve the sherbet in scoops on dessert plates, decorated with chopped figs.

Strawberries and Balsamic Cream

This simple dessert was a favorite of many expatriates living in France.

⅓ cup/75 ml balsamic vinegar

2 teaspoons plus 4 tablespoons sugar (divided)

½ teaspoon freshly squeezed lemon juice

½ cup/100 g mascarpone cheese or cream cheese, chilled

½ cup/120 ml whipping cream, chilled

1 teaspoon vanilla extract

3 x 1-pint baskets/1.5 kg strawberries, hulled and halved

SERVES 4

Combine the vinegar, 2 teaspoons of sugar, and the lemon juice in a small, heavy saucepan. Stir over medium heat until the sugar dissolves, then boil until the syrup is reduced to a scant ¼ cup/60 ml, about 3 minutes. Transfer to a small bowl; cool completely. (This can be made 2 days ahead, in which case cover and refrigerate until ready to use.)

Combine the mascarpone or cream cheese, cream, vanilla, and 2 tablespoons of sugar in a medium bowl. Whisk until soft peaks form. Cover and refrigerate for up to 4 hours.

Combine the strawberries and the remaining 2 tablespoons of sugar in a large bowl. Drizzle with the balsamic syrup and toss to blend. Let stand for 30 minutes, stirring occasionally.

Divide the strawberries and syrup among four dishes and top with the mascarpone mixture.

Cherry Clafoutis

Popular in the south of France, Clafoutis is the sort of dessert that shows a rustic side of French cuisine, while also being something that you want to enjoy and savor at leisure. If cherries are not your favorite (I'm sure Zelda Fitzgerald would have preferred peach), feel free to use any stone fruit or berry.

2 cups/300 g canned tart cherries, drained (or use fresh cherries)

¼ cup/60 ml brandy

⅔ cup/130 g sugar

cooking spray

1 cup/235 ml milk

⅔ cup/90 g all-purpose/plain flour, sifted

3 large eggs

1 tablespoon vanilla extract

1 tablespoon lemon zest

¼ teaspoon salt

⅛ teaspoon allspice

1 teaspoon confectioner's/icing sugar, or as needed

SERVES 6–8

Mix the cherries, brandy, and half the sugar in a bowl; let soak for 1 hour.

Preheat the oven to 450°F (230°C) Gas 8. Spray a 9-in/23-cm pie pan with cooking spray.

Remove the cherries from the brandy mixture using a slotted spoon and transfer to the prepared pie pan. Pour the brandy mixture into the bowl of a mixer, add the remaining sugar, milk, flour, eggs, vanilla extract, lemon zest, salt, and allspice. Blend until well combined and the mixture is smooth. Pour the batter over the cherries in the pan.

Bake in the preheated oven for 5 minutes, then reduce the heat to 350°F (175°C) Gas 4 and continue baking for 45–50 minutes until golden and puffy. Cool slightly and dust with confectioner's/icing sugar to serve.

Chapter Seven
Drinks

The Bee's Knees

The Gin Rickey

The French 75

Between the Sheets

The Rose Cocktail

Villa America Special

The Bailey

The Franklin

Dorothy Parker Champagne Punch

The Bee's Knees

This Prohibition-era cocktail was popular during the 1920s—not just because it's a good concoction, but because the honey and the lemon and orange juice greatly hid the smell of liquor. The juice is optional. Bars in Los Angeles and New York that serve The Bee's Knees omit it, but it was most likely included during the Jazz Age.

4 tablespoons honey

4 tablespoons hot water

3 fl oz/90 ml gin

1 tablespoon freshly squeezed lemon juice

1 tablespoon freshly squeezed orange juice

ice

twists of lemon, to serve

SERVES 4

Mix the honey and hot water together to make a syrup. Combine all the ingredients and shake well with ice. Strain into a martini or rocks glass and serve with a twist.

The Gin Rickey

Tom Buchanan mixes four of these cocktails up for his wife Daisy, Nick Carraway, Jordan Baker, and Gatsby in *The Great Gatsby* after Daisy instructs him to "make us a cold drink." Tom returns, "preceding four gin rickeys that clicked full of ice."

ice

2 fl oz/60 ml freshly squeezed lime juice

8 fl oz/235 ml London dry gin

2 limes, cut in half

club soda/soda water

SERVES 4

Fill four Collins glasses full of ice. Pour equal amounts of lime juice into each glass. Add the gin to each glass, throw in a lime half, and top up with bubbly water of choice.

The French 75

Said to be a favorite drink of Fitzgerald and also, on occasion, Hemingway, this cocktail is named after a 75mm (3 inch) MI 1857 gun used in World War I. The recipe combines Champagne, gin, sugar, and lemon juice.

1 cup/200 g sugar

ice

4 fl oz/120 ml gin or Cognac

2 fl oz/60 ml freshly squeezed lemon juice

8 fl oz/235 ml Champagne

twists of lemon, to serve

SERVES 4

First make a simple syrup. In a saucepan over low heat, warm the sugar with 1 cup/235 ml water until dissolved. Cool to room temperature before using. (There will be extra syrup; refrigerate if not using immediately.)

In a cocktail shaker filled with ice, shake the gin or Cognac, lemon juice, and ½ fl oz/15 ml simple syrup. Strain into chilled flutes or cocktail coupes. Top with Champagne and garnish with lemon twists.

Between the Sheets

This drink, a popular take on the Sidecar (but using rum) was rumored to be the drink of choice for prostitutes at Parisian brothels during the 1920s. Its creation is usually attributed to the renowned barman Harry MacElhone at the infamous Harry's Bar in Paris. In *The Great Gatsby*, Nick joins Tom Buchanan for an afternoon in New York City. As they embark on this journey, he is not aware that they will also be joined by Tom's mistress, Myrtle. After a long day of drinking, Mr McKee, a minor character described as a "pale, feminine man," ends up "between the sheets," an encounter that has elicited much speculation.

4 fl oz/120 ml white rum

4 fl oz/120 ml Cointreau

2 fl oz/60 ml freshly squeezed lemon juice

4 fl oz/120 ml cognac

ice

twists of orange peel, to serve

SERVES 4

Shake the rum, Cointreau, lemon juice, and cognac (you can substitute another French or Spanish brandy for a softer version) well with cracked ice, then strain into four chilled cocktail glasses and garnish with a twist of orange peel.

Drunk Before Noon

When we think of the expat community in the Paris of the 1920s, we typically think of artists, musicians, and writers, but they were not the only people seeking a place more sympathetic to their creativity. When Prohibition started making its mark on the United States in 1920, some of the greatest mixologists in New York and Chicago hopped on the ocean liners bound for France to ply their trade, and to learn a few tricks from their French counterparts.

The resulting fusion of American and French know-how made Paris a top-notch center of cocktail culture. And what could be better for a lonely exile in Paris than to find a friendly fellow American behind the bar, ready to listen to your sorrows and pour you a stiff drink?

Notable bartenders who emigrated and became, at least temporarily, Parisians included Frank Meier of the Ritz Carlton New York and Fernand "Pete" Petiot of Harry's New York Bar. With their arrival, Paris underwent a cocktail renaissance.

The American cocktail culture was something new for Parisians; in France, alcohol was primarily drunk with and after meals to aid digestion, and although the French enjoyed wine, strong spirits did not sit so well with them. Americans gave the Parisians cocktails such as the Bloody Mary, the French 75, and the Sidecar; Fitzgerald was able to get a good Mint Julep, and Cole Porter could find his perfect Bourbon after a long night of playing. In return, Paris supplied traditional tonics, elixirs, and cordials to boost the mixers' creativity.

By catering to both French and American tastes, these American-turned-French bartenders were able to keep their bars full of happy customers— the perfect riposte to the restrictions of Prohibition that they had left behind.

Alcohol was, of course, a defining feature of Fitzgerald's life, and also his work. Like many of his fellow Americans in Paris, Fitzgerald drank often and at all times of day, but as his career progressed, drinking began to dominate his work. From the hell-raisers who attended Gatsby's parties to the seemingly perfect couple in *The Beautiful and Damned*, Fitzgerald's writing became filled with privileged but haunted souls whose lives were soaked in alcohol. After years of heavy drinking, Fitzgerald would die at the early age of 44, from a heart attack.

American Bar "Le Select", on the Champs Elysées in Paris

The Rose Cocktail

A popular cocktail in 1920s' Paris, this delicate concoction gets its soft pink color from the addition of raspberry syrup, and its floral notes from the use of French vermouth and kirsch, a dry cherry liqueur.

8 fl oz/235 ml French vermouth

4 fl oz/120 ml kirsch (cherry brandy)

4 teaspoons raspberry syrup, such as Monin

ice

4 maraschino cherries, to garnish

SERVES 4

In two batches, combine the vermouth, kirsch, and syrup in a cocktail shaker filled with ice; cover and shake until chilled, about 15 seconds. Strain into chilled martini glasses and add a cherry to serve.

Villa America Special
aka The Sidecar

The Villa America was the house cocktail of Gerald and Sara Murphy, the Fitzgeralds' friends, partners in crime, and also the inspiration behind Dick and Nicole Diver, two of F. Scott Fitzgerald's most famous literary creations. This cocktail is named after their villa in the south of France.

3 fl oz/90 ml freshly squeezed lemon juice

granulated sugar

6 fl oz/180 ml Pierre Ferrand Cognac

4 fl oz/120 ml liqueur (such as Cointreau, or another liqueur of your choosing)

ice

SERVES 4

Chill the cocktail glasses. Rub the rims of the glasses with lemon, then dip in granulated sugar. In two batches, shake the cognac, liqueur, and lemon juice well with ice, then strain into chilled glasses.

The Bailey

The gin-based Bailey was the favored drink of Gerald Murphy, well-known American socialite and lifelong friend of Fitzgerald, who was also said to enjoy this refreshing drink regularly.

1 ¾ cups/400ml gin

sprigs of fresh mint

8 tablespoons freshly squeezed grapefruit juice

8 tablespoons freshly squeezed lime juice

ice

Serves 4

Put the gin and some torn mint sprigs in an ice-filled shaker. Shake, then distribute evenly among glasses. Add the grapefruit and lime juices, stir, and garnish each with a whole mint sprig.

The Franklin

When it comes to a Dirty Martini, it's always a toss-up between using vodka or gin. This Prohibition-era cocktail goes for gin. Most people would have ordered it simply as a "Gin Martini," but it was officially dubbed The Franklin after US President Franklin D. Roosevelt repealed Prohibition. Especially fitting, seeing as it was his drink of choice.
If you want to make more than two Franklins, for the best results just make more in batches—don't fill the shaker with more than two servings at a time.

ice

3 fl oz/90 ml dry gin

1 fl oz/30 ml dry vermouth

2½ fl oz/75 ml olive juice

6 olives, skewered

Serves 2

Fill a shaker with ice. Pour the gin, vermouth, and olive juice into the shaker and shake vigorously. Shake it like it owes you money! Pour into two martini glasses and serve with the olive garnish.

Dorothy Parker Champagne Punch

This was a popular Champagne punch during the 1920s, named in honor of the witty American poet and critic. It would have likely been served at many of the elaborate and not so elaborate parties attended by the band of American writers forging their reputation at that time.

2 bottles of Champagne

2 tablespoons orange Curaçao

4 tablespoons brandy

2 cups/400 g sugar

2 cups/475 ml rum

juice from two freshly squeezed lemons

1 cup/235 ml pineapple juice

1 cup/235 ml tea, cooled
(use black, green, or chamomile tea)

club soda/soda water, to serve

Serves 4–6

Mix the ingredients together in a large punch bowl with 1 cup/235 ml water, then top with soda water before serving.

Timeline

1896	Francis Scott Key Fitzgerald is born on September 24, to parents Edward and Mary Fitzgerald (née McQuillan), in St Paul, Minnesota, USA.
1908	He is sent to St Paul Academy, but in 1911 he is moved to the Newman School, a Catholic prep school in New Jersey.
1913	Graduates from the Newman School. Continues his education at Princeton University, and writes scripts for the Triangle Club musicals, as well as articles for magazines.
1917	Drops out of Princeton to join the US Army. Assigned to Camp Sheridan, near Montgomery in Alabama, USA. Meets 18-year-old Zelda Sayre, daughter of an Alabama Supreme Court justice.
1918	World War One ends in November, before Fitzgerald is deployed. Discharged from the Army, he moves to New York to work in advertising, but quits after a few months and returns to St Paul to rewrite his first novel, *The Romantic Egoist*, which would become *This Side of Paradise*.
1920	*This Side of Paradise* is published and receives great reviews. One week later Fitzgerald marries Zelda in New York.
1921	The Fitzgeralds have a daughter, Frances Scott Fitzgerald, known as Scottie.
1922	Fitzgerald's second novel, *The Beautiful and Damned*, is published.
1924	The Fitzgeralds move to France, and Scott completes *The Great Gatsby*.
1925	Fitzgerald meets Ernest Hemingway in Paris, and through Hemingway he is introduced to the expat community. *The Great Gatsby* is published.
1926–1930	The Fitzgeralds move backward and forward between Europe (especially France) and America. Zelda's mental health declines and Fitzgerald's drinking increases. He also suffers from writer's block.

1927	Works for United Artists as a screenwriter.
1930	Suffering another breakdown, Zelda is treated at a hospital in Maryland, and later that year she is admitted to a clinic in Switzerland.
1931	Fitzgerald works for Metro-Goldwyn-Mayer as a writer, until spring of 1932.
1934	Fitzgerald's fourth novel, *Tender Is the Night*, is published. It is not well received on first publication.
1937	Fitzgerald moves to Hollywood to revive his career as a screenwriter. Begins a relationship with gossip columnist Sheilah Graham, while still married to Zelda.
1939	Begins work on another novel, *The Love of the Last Tycoon*.
1940	On December 21, 1940, Fitzgerald has a heart attack and dies, at the age of 44, in Hollywood.
1941	*The Last Tycoon*, Fitzgerald's last and uncompleted novel, is published posthumously.
1948	Zelda dies in a fire at the Highland Hospital in Asheville, North Carolina, where she is a patient.

Further reading

Dates of first publication are given in brackets, other editions have been published since then in most cases.

F. Scott Fitzgerald
This Side of Paradise (1920)
The Beautiful and Damned (1922)
The Great Gatsby (1925)
Tender Is the Night (1934)
The Last Tycoon or The Love of the Last Tycoon (1941)

Zelda Fitzgerald
The Collected Writings of Zelda Fitzgerald (1991, 1997)
Save Me the Waltz (1932)

James Beard
Hors d'Oeuvres and Canapés (1940)

Auguste Escoffier
Ma Cuisine (1907)

Ernest Hemingway
A Moveable Feast (1964)

Marcel Proust
In Search of Lost Time or À la Recherche du Temps Perdu (1913–27)

James Joyce
Ulysses (1922)

Gertrude Stein
Tender Buttons (1914)
The Autobiography of Alice B. Toklas (1933)

Alice B. Toklas
The Alice B. Toklas Cookbook (1954)

Oscar Wilde
"The Importance of Being Earnest" (1895)

Index

Picture credits

Susan Bell: p. 52

Martin Brigdale: pp. 54, 106, 125

Peter Cassidy: p. 35, 109, 142, 148

Getty Images/American Stock Archive: p. 7

Getty Images/Apic: pp. 61, 153

Getty Images/Albert Harlingue: p. 145

Getty Images/Hulton Archive/Stringer: pp. 21, 115

Getty Images/Mondadori Portfolio: p. 6

Getty Images/Photo 12: p. 39

Getty Images/Topical Press Agency / Stringer: p. 85

Richard Jung: p. 126

William Lingwood: p. 93

Alex Luck: pp. 1–5, 8–16, 18–19, 23–31, 33–34, 36–37, 41–48,
51–59, 63–75, 81–83, 86–91, 95–98, 100–103, 107, 110–114,
116–124, 127–141, 143, 147, 149–151, 157

Diana Miller: p. 76

Gloria Nicol: pp. 99, 105

Steve Painter: p. 17

William Reavell: pp.78, 104, 146

Claire Richardson: p. 32

Stuart West: p. 50

Acknowledgments

When raising a child, there is an old proverb that, "it takes a village".
It's a similar sort of process when creating a book. The author gets all the
credit, when in reality, there are so many people that deserve just as much,
if not more credit. This is a book that has been the cause of many long nights,
many brainstorming sessions, and many hours of research.

This book would be nothing without the team behind it. My thanks and
gratitude are more than I could ever express and I am honored to have worked
alongside such talented people. Thank you to Louise Leffler, the brilliant and
creative designer behind the look of this book; I'd also like to thank Luis Peral, the
stylist for giving this cookbook some swagger. To Sue Henderson and her team
of Loic Parisot and Sian Henley—the food stylists and visionaries—I can't say
enough how good a job this turned out. Thank you so much. And to the real star,
Alex Luck, whose keen eye and brilliant photography brought it all to life;
I think Fitzgerald would approve.

At the end of the day, this book would be nothing without its editors,
Gillian Haslam and Nathan Joyce. They do amazing work, not just with this title,
but with so many others published by CICO Books and RPS, past and present.
A special thanks to Miriam Catley for her patience and keen eye to detail,
to Cindy Richards, for allowing me to work on this project, and last but not least,
to Penny Craig. She knows how to put together a great team.

Finally, I'd like to thank F. Scott and Zelda Fitzgerald. They were two truly
outrageous individuals who, among an array of other eclectic souls, carved
out an interesting time in history, culture—and food.